World of Reading

A Thematic Approach to Reading Comprehension

2

Joan Baker-González
University of Puerto Rico, Mayagüez (retired)

Eileen K. Blau
University of Puerto Rico, Mayagüez

PEARSON
Longman

World of Reading 2
A Thematic Approach to Reading Comprehension

Pearson Education, 10 Bank Street, White Plains, NY 10606

Acknowledgments: There are many to be thanked for helping us in the process of developing the *World of Reading* series. First and foremost is the University of Puerto Rico at Mayagüez (UPRM) for granting Dr. Blau a sabbatical leave that enabled her to give this project the attention it needed. We are also grateful to the English Department at UPRM, in particular Dr. Betsy Morales, Director, who has supported us in every way possible. We would like to thank the following colleagues, former colleagues, friends, and family members who have generously supported us in the process of developing these books. Those who have helped us in locating appropriate reading selections to use in the series are: Dorothy Blau, Emily Graeser, John Green, Leonora Hamilton, Anthony Hunt, Jeannette Lugo, Rosita Rivera, and Prisca Rodríguez. We would also like to thank the following people for sharing their expertise with us: Eric Blau, Gary Breckon, William Frey, Kenneth Lewis, Aliette Marcelin, Susan Niemeyer, Patricia Payne, Aixa Rodríguez, Robert W. Smith, and Dr. Christa Von Hilldebrandt. We are especially grateful to Steven Neufeld and Ali Billuroglu for helping us use their valuable vocabulary profiler at the Compleat Lexical Tutor website. And of course we are grateful to the staff at Pearson Longman who have helped us along the way: Laura LeDréan who got us started, Wendy Campbell, Jaime Lieber, Danielle Belfiore, Adina Zoltan, Paula Van Ells, Pietro Alongi, and our development editor, Stacey Hunter. And finally, we wish to thank the writers whose work constitutes the core of these books, as well as all the students we have had over the years who have helped us learn about teaching English language learners to be good readers.

Staff credits: The people who made up the *World of Reading 2* team, representing editorial, production, design, and manufacturing, are Pietro Alongi, Danielle Belfiore, Dave Dickey, Christine Edmonds, Oliva Fernandez, Stacey Hunter, Jaime Lieber, Paula Van Ells, Pat Wosczyk, and Adina Zoltan.

Text composition: Integra Software Services Pvt. Ltd.
Text font: 11/13 Minion
Illustrations and tech art: Dan Rosandich and Kenneth Batelman
Text and photo credits: See page 182.

Library of Congress Cataloging-in-Publication Data
Baker-González, Joan.
   World of reading/Joan Baker-González, Eileen K. Blau.
     p. cm.
   Rev. ed. of two previous publications: Building on basics, 1999 and Building understanding, 1995.
   ISBN 978-0-13-600244-4 (student book 1)—ISBN 978-0-13-600210-9 (teacher's ed. 1)—
ISBN 978-0-13-600211-6 (student book 2)—ISBN 978-0-13-600212-3 (teacher's ed. 2)—
ISBN 978-0-13-600214-7 (student book 3)—ISBN 978-0-13-600215-4 (teacher's ed. 3) 1. English language—Textbooks for foreign speakers. 2. Reading comprehension—Problems, exercises, etc. 3. Readers. I. Blau, Eileen K. II. Baker-González, Joan. Building on basics. III. Baker-González, Joan. Building understanding. IV. Title.
   PE1128.B274 2009
   428.0076—dc22

2008034098

ISBN-13: 978-0-13-600211-6
ISBN-10: 0-13-600211-0

PEARSON LONGMAN ON THE WEB

Pearsonlongman.com offers online resources for teachers and students. Access our Companion Websites, our online catalog, and our local offices around the world.

Visit us at **www.pearsonlongman.com**.

Printed in the United States of America
4 5 6 7 8 9 10—V064—13 12 11 10

Contents

Scope and Sequence

UNIT	CHAPTER	TITLE AND GENRE	READING AND STUDY SKILLS*
	Student's Introduction		Highlighting important information
1 Growing Up	1	My Early Memories *autobiography*	Predicting paragraph content Recognizing reasons
	2	Peer Influences on Achievement *book excerpt*	Writer's purpose Understanding research Topic and main idea
	3	It's OK to Be Different *personal essay*	Cause and effect Topic and main idea
	4	To a Daughter Leaving Home *poem*	Reading poetry: images, simile, and metaphor
Unit Wrap-Up			
2 Between Two Worlds	5	People on the Move: Moving Young *report*	Getting information from graphs and statistics Highlighting or note-taking
	6	Bibi and Rajini *personal stories based on interviews*	Reading summary blurb and choosing selection Sharing information Highlighting or note-taking
	7	Bosnia's Loss Is an American City's Gain *newspaper article*	Organizing information into a chart Highlighting or note-taking
	8	(Un)American *excerpt from personal essay*	Topic and main idea
Unit Wrap-Up			

*All chapters practice the following skills which are not repeated in the Scope and Sequence: **Activating background knowledge, Previewing, Determining a purpose for reading, Inferring meaning of vocabulary while reading,** and **Supporting answers with evidence from the reading.**

VOCABULARY SKILLS	FOUNDATIONS FOR WRITING
Using a glossary Synonyms	
Synonyms	

Synonyms
British English
	Creating strong effect
	  with few words
	Absence of author's
	  voice

Word families
Collocations
Unit glossary
	Gathering and
	  organizing information
	  before writing
	Using statistics and
	  information from
	  graphs in writing

Synonyms Multiword expressions	The narrative present
	Paragraph topics
Handling non-essential vocabulary	

Word families
Words with more than one meaning
	Gathering and
	  organizing information
	  before writing
	Paragraph writing

Teacher's Introduction

ABOUT *WORLD OF READING*

World of Reading, a multi-genre thematic reading series, is a revision and expansion of the successful *Building on Basics* and *Building Understanding* books. The new, more streamlined three-book series has updated reading selections that are engaging and varied, and a vocabulary program built on current research and the results of vocabulary profiler analysis. The careful selection of complementary thematic readings and the research-based focus on vocabulary building give students a solid foundation for academic reading.

The Readings

Central to the increased academic focus is the variety of texts in the new series.

- Texts are authentic, written for native speakers of English, moving from adapted to non-adapted.
- Texts cover a broad spectrum of topics common in college level courses including science, social science, business, and literature.
- Each book has at least one selection from a textbook.
- Each book has readings that report on research.
- Some selections are contemporary and some are older, encouraging students to develop historical perspective.

Vocabulary Building

To select vocabulary for the stronger vocabulary component, every reading was analyzed using tools at the Compleat Lexical Tutor website. Reading selections were submitted to the vocabulary profiler developed by Billuroglu and Neufeld, the BNL, as well as the Classic version of the British National Corpus vocabulary profiler, to reveal the words on the Academic Word List—the AWL (Coxhead 2000).[*] In all cases we began with authentic readings, but in Book 1, we adapted most of them so that 90–95% of the vocabulary can be found on the list of the 2000 most frequent words. Book 2 has minimally adapted texts while texts in Book 3 are unadapted and thus entirely authentic.

Facts concerning vocabulary and reading length are summarized as follows:

World of Reading 1: Targeted vocabulary is generally chosen from words that are less common than the first 2,000 words of English, selected AWL words and multiword expressions. Selections are approximately 400–800 words.

World of Reading 2: Most targeted vocabulary also comes from words that are less common than the first 2,000 words, but since these readings are minimally adapted, there is a heavier vocabulary load. Again, selected AWL words and multiword expressions are targeted. Selections are approximately 500–1,200 words.

*Coxhead, Averil (2000). A New Academic Word List. *TESOL Quarterly* 34:2 (213–238).

World of Reading 3: Targeted vocabulary is generally chosen from words that are less frequent than the 2,500 most frequent words, selected AWL words, and multiword expressions. Selections are usually 800 words or longer.

World of Reading serves as a foundation for academic work and presents teachers with various opportunities to foster an academic mindset in their students. Thus, exercises in this series encourage students to:

- support answers to questions with evidence from the text
- develop the ability to distinguish a writer's ideas from one's personal opinions of them
- give writers and researchers credit for their ideas
- be curious about the world, its problems and their solutions

Description of the Books

Each book consists of six units that focus on a topic of personal or world interest. The units have four chapters, each with one reading plus exercises. The first three chapters of each unit are non-fiction—usually magazine, newspaper or Internet articles, or excerpts from non-fiction books, such as content area textbooks. The fourth selection is a piece of literature—a short story, a poem, a personal essay, or an excerpt from an autobiography or memoir. The literature selections are not adapted.

To benefit from a thematic reader, students must read several selections on a single topic. When determining what to include in a reading program, it's important to think in terms of whole units rather than individual reading selections. Omitting a single selection from a unit would probably leave enough material for students to benefit from related readings, but choosing a single reading from a unit would not. Also, when choosing selections remember that the non-fiction selections tend to build background knowledge that facilitates the comprehension and enjoyment of the literature selections.

Each book begins with a Student's Introductory Chapter that is designed to introduce students to important features of the book. It should not be omitted. In the back of the book, you will find maps of the world and North America. It has been our experience that a teacher can't count on students knowing geography, and we suggest you use this series to improve students' knowledge of the world. Talk with them about the many places mentioned in *World of Reading* and find out what they know about them.

Organization of the Units

Units and chapters of *World of Reading* follow a consistent format, making it easier for students and teachers to use the series.

The title, picture(s), questions, and quote(s) on the **Unit Opener** can all be used to activate students' background knowledge of the unit topic as well as to make predictions about its content. However, do not expect students to have more than partial answers to the questions until they have completed the unit.

The material in **About the Reading** varies in length and content depending on the reading; it contains information about the source of the reading, occasionally background information on the topic, and especially in the case of literary selections, information about the author. We suggest that you talk to students about the fact that the source of material is of interest and value in the academic world.

Before You Read usually includes two parts: **Thinking about the Topic** and **Previewing**. These are designed to activate students' background knowledge for the chapter. Sometimes vocabulary that is essential for comprehension of the reading is introduced before students read; in this case, it is italicized. You may find these words in the Vocabulary Review exercise described below.

Good readers generally preview non-fiction material. Therefore, we provide practice of this skill for non-fiction selections. Previewing gives readers an idea of what to expect and, consequently, a better chance to understand. In most cases the whole class should do these parts together.

Another important reading skill that comes before reading is **having a purpose for reading**. Students are regularly instructed to turn to the questions in Comprehension Check – First Reading. Being able to answer the two or three questions in that exercise provides a purpose for the first reading.

A new feature of this series is what we call **marginal multiple choice (MMC)**. It provides help in inferring at least partial meanings of words while reading. In the margin next to a word or expression that is likely to be unfamiliar but which is partially inferable, students will see two choices, only one of which makes sense in the context. Encourage students to take advantage of this unique feature so they can continue reading more fluently when the vocabulary load is heavy for them.

Another feature that helps students to continue reading is **glossing**. The following types of items are typically glossed: culturally specific and technical terms, proper names, foreign words and phrases, acronyms and abbreviations, slang terms, archaic vocabulary, and occasionally some difficult vocabulary that is not important for students to learn at their current level. For the poems, difficult vocabulary is glossed so students can read them easily and with maximum enjoyment.

Students will read each selection twice; **Comprehension Check – First Reading** is a short set of questions that students should be able to answer after finishing the first reading of a selection. The questions are text-bound and require a basic comprehension of the whole text; they cannot be answered simply by reading the beginning of the selection.

Comprehension Check – Second Reading requires more thorough understanding but still focuses on the text and its meaning as opposed to students' opinions of it. Formats include true/false, multiple choice, matching, listing, filling in charts, sorting, and the more traditional *wh*-questions. When responding to this exercise, students should always be required to support their answers with evidence from the text. There are good reasons for doing this:

- Having students explain how they arrived at an answer or a conclusion can help teachers see where comprehension is weak, and enables them to guide students onto the right track if necessary.
- Sometimes students see things in the text that we may have overlooked. For example, teachers may not notice ambiguities that students do notice, and what appears to be an "incorrect" answer might actually be supported by evidence from the text.

Starting in Book 2, you will sometimes find a note-taking icon in **Comprehension Check – Second Reading** when there are *wh*-questions. When this icon appears, students are instructed to highlight or jot down facts, words and phrases, but not complete sentences (at least not without using quotation marks). The purpose is to develop an important academic skill, note-taking, and the instruction not to copy whole sentences is an opportunity to begin teaching students to be careful about plagiarism. Whatever the form of the comprehension check, its primary purpose is to help students develop the ability to read and learn from authentic texts on their own, not to test their comprehension.

Vocabulary exercises follow all readings except poems. Target vocabulary includes words that are pre-taught in Thinking about the Topic, that have marginal multiple choices, and that appear in Vocabulary Building exercises. These are listed by chapter at the back of the book. The vocabulary exercises in this program are intended to give students help in learning the meanings of the numerous words and expressions that they will encounter in authentic texts. Given that it takes multiple exposures to learn new words and expressions, and the fact that there are so many polysemous words in the language, we strongly recommend that vocabulary exercises be seen as an opportunity for teaching rather than testing. We also hope you will encourage your students to keep a word bank as described in the Student's Introductory Chapter of each book.

The first vocabulary exercise in each chapter is marginal multiple choice. The key goal in this exercise is for students to get partial meaning and to be able to continue reading. The first after-reading vocabulary exercise is Vocabulary Building, in which words and expressions are presented in the exact context in which they are used in the selection. The second exercise, provided in nearly half the chapters, helps students use the steps described in the Student's Introductory Chapter to Book 1: recognizing and skipping non-essential vocabulary; noticing and learning multiword expressions as single units; locating definitions in the text; inferring from context and using prefixes, suffixes, and the parts of compound words to figure out their meaning; and practicing dictionary use.

The last vocabulary exercise, **Vocabulary Review**, is a cloze exercise that draws on vocabulary in the previous exercises, multiple choice vocabulary checks from the margins next to the readings, and words introduced in the **Before You Read** section. This exercise gives additional exposure to some of the targeted vocabulary, an important factor in vocabulary acquisition. It also provides a summary of the selection, which can help improve comprehension and can serve as a model for summarizing, if you choose to use it that way.

Please note that several units in the series include a glossary of technical terms related to the unit topic. This new academic feature mirrors content area textbooks and helps students expand their vocabularies.

Text Analysis exercises help students derive meaning from a selection, notice elements that can aid their reading comprehension and teach them some things that will help them with their own writing. Many of the exercises in this section involve looking at overall organization of texts, revealing ways in which texts are commonly organized by North American and British writers. Other exercises focus on smaller segments of text down to the word level. Elements of literature and conventions of academic writing are the focus of a few Text Analysis exercises.

Responding to Reading offers discussion questions that relate closely to the text but extend to broader, related issues, allowing students to talk about their own personal experience and opinions. These questions allow students to engage in the academic practice of developing and discussing ideas on a topic they now know something about. When doing this section, you can foster vocabulary acquisition by listing vocabulary items on the chalkboard and encouraging students to use them in their discussion.

The **Unit Wrap-Up** has two major components: **Extending Your Vocabulary** and **Writing**. Extending Your Vocabulary recycles vocabulary from the unit and has two parts. The first part is **Word Families**, which extends vocabulary knowledge by teaching related words; it also sensitizes students to parts of speech and derivational suffixes. The second is either **Words with More Than One Meaning** (**Polysemous Words** in Book 3) or **Collocations**. The former calls attention to other meanings of words seen in the unit; the latter focuses attention on how native speakers combine words and thus leads learners to speak and write more like native English speakers. These exercises provide additional exposure to reinforce vocabulary acquisition while helping to refine and deepen word knowledge.

The Writing section offers further opportunity for thinking about the topic and issues raised in the unit. It allows students to express themselves, to try to use new vocabulary, and to learn some of the fundamentals of clear writing for both test-taking situations and success in future writing courses.

Flexibility in Ordering Exercises and Grouping Students

Varying the order of exercises for a selection might be advantageous for your students. For example, it might be beneficial to do Vocabulary Building exercises between the first and second readings. In this way students can benefit from a stronger awareness of vocabulary and sensitivity to context during their second reading. The Vocabulary Review, however, should be done later because it serves the dual purpose of reviewing vocabulary and summarizing the selection itself. It may also be helpful to do a Text Analysis exercise before the second reading, especially when the exercise provides an overview of how the entire selection is organized. Final decisions about ordering of exercises are best made by you, the teacher.

With regard to grouping your students for doing the exercises, use your judgment concerning whether it would be best to have students work in pairs, small groups, as a whole class, or individually.

Teacher's Manual with Tests

There is a Teacher's Manual to accompany each book. It includes answer keys, a few tips for teachers, recommended readings and websites and a unit test. Unit Tests have two sections: Reviewing, which focuses on the vocabulary and content of the unit and Exploring, which consists of a new authentic reading on the unit topic with vocabulary and comprehension questions. The new reading in the test can also be used as instructional material if you prefer.

* * *

We hope that both you and your students find this series a helpful and enjoyable way for students to increase their ability to read authentic texts and ultimately to succeed in their academic endeavors.

Student's Introductory Chapter

GETTING STARTED WITH *WORLD OF READING 2*

In this short chapter we will show you some techniques to make you a better reader of English. You will use them with all the readings in this book.

Before You Read

Before reading the selected texts in each chapter, you will think about the material and talk about it. Then you will preview the material—look at headings, the first paragraph, the first sentence of each paragraph, and any photos, charts, tables, etc., and their captions. You will also focus on your purpose for reading the selection by reading the Comprehension Check questions before you begin.

While You Read

The readings in this book have not been substantially adapted for English language learners, so you can expect to find unfamiliar words—probably too many to look up in your dictionary, especially as you read something for the first time. To deal with new words and expressions while you read, we suggest you follow these five basic steps, which were explained in detail in the Student's Introductory Chapter of *World of Reading 1*: **1**. Locate the problem. **2**. Decide if the word or phrase is important or not. **3**. Look for a definition in the text. **4A**. Check the parts of the word. **4B**. Check the context. **5**. Get help—use your dictionary.

We will now use the first paragraph of the first reading in Unit 1, "My Early Memories," to review these five steps for dealing with unfamiliar vocabulary, particularly Steps 1 and 2.

Step 1: Locate the Problem

Is it a single word or a multiword expression (MWE)? Perhaps one of the most difficult things for a nonnative speaker of English is to recognize MWEs as meaningful units. There are two in this paragraph: *take care of* and *care about*.

a. Gram Alice McKoy, my maternal grandmother, was *taking care of* me, since both my parents worked.

b. My keenest memory of that day is not of the shock and pain, but of feeling important, being the center of attention, seeing how much they loved and *cared about* me.

The word *care* occurs in both of these sentences. The central meaning of the word *care* is illustrated in the sentence: "I care about learning English." In other words, it is important to me.

Note in the dictionary entries below that there are many other meanings for *care*, both alone and in MWEs.

In example (a), the problem is not the word *care* but the MWE *take care of.* Scan the dictionary entries below to see if you find the expression. Which meaning of *take care of* fits this context?

In example (b), *care* is a verb followed by the preposition *about*. Look at the verb entry for *care*. There is an example sentence with *care* followed by *about*. "He doesn't care about anybody but himself." This example sentence says, "Nobody is important to him except himself." In Powell's example sentence (b), you have the same expression, but with a positive meaning—"He was important to his family."

care¹ /ker/ v. [I,T] to be concerned about or interested in someone or something: *He doesn't **care about** anybody but himself.* | *I don't **care what** you do.*

SPOKEN PHRASES

1 who cares? Used in order to say in an impolite way that you do not care about something because you do not think it is important **2 I/he/they etc. couldn't care less** used in order to say in an impolite way that someone does not care at all about something **3 what do I/you/they etc. care?** Used in order to say in an impolite way that some one does not care at all about something: *What does he care? He'll get his money whatever happens.* **4** FORMAL to like or want something: ***Would you care to meet us after the show?*** | *I don't really **care for** peanuts.*

care for sb/sth phr v [T] **1** to help someone when s/he is sick or not able to do things for himself/herself: *Angie **cared for** her mother after her stroke.* **2** to do things to keep something in good condition or working correctly: *instructions on **caring for** your new sofa*

care² n.

1 ►HELP◄ [U] the process of helping someone who is sick or not able to do things for himself/ herself: *Your father will need constant medical care.* | *the care of young children*

2 ►LOOKING AFTER STH◄ [U] the process of doing things to something so that it stays in good condition and works correctly: *With proper care, your washing machine should last years.*

3 take care of a) to watch and help someone: *Who's taking care of the baby?* **b)** to do things to keep something in good condition or working correctly: *Karl will take care of the house while we're on vacation.* **c)** to do the work or make the arrangements that are necessary for something to happen: *I'll take care of making the reservations.* **d)** to pay for something: *Don't worry about the bill, it's taken care of.*

4 ►CAREFULNESS◄ [U] carefulness to avoid damage, mistakes etc.: *Handle the package **with care.*** | *You'd better put more care into your work!*

5 ►WORRY◄ [C,U] feelings of worry, concern, or unhappiness: *Eddie **doesn't have a care in the world.*** (=doesn't have any problems or worries)

6 take care a) SPOKEN used when saying goodbye to family or friends **b)** to be careful: *It's very icy, so take care driving home.*

7 care of used when sending letters to someone at someone else's address: *Just send the package to me care of my cousin.*

Notice all of the uses and expressions that you can learn if you study these dictionary entries.

Recognizing a MWE can be a problem. One hint we can give you is that if one word alone doesn't make sense to you, look at the words before and after it. Could two or more words go together to form a unit of meaning? With time, you will become more aware of phrasal verbs and other MWEs.

Step 2: Distinguishing Essential from Non-essential Words and Expressions

The next step is to decide if the word or expression is essential (important) or not, particularly in the first reading. If it is not essential, keep reading. If it is essential, follow Steps 3–5. Remember that general or partial meaning is often enough.

This book, like *World of Reading 1*, has a special feature that helps you use context (Step 4B) to infer at least partial meaning, so you can keep reading. For some words that may be unfamiliar, you will see two choices (a. and b.) in the margin to the right of the word. Ask yourself which makes sense in the context; that meaning will be enough.

Turn to page 3. Read the first paragraph of "My Early Memories" without stopping, except to mark or list the words and expressions you don't know.

You may wonder how to determine which of the words or expressions you marked is essential or non-essential. When you are reading a narrative, you want to be able to answer the following questions: *Who is in the story? What happened? Where and when did the incident take place? What is important about this story?* In writing that is not a narrative, you need to ask yourself, *What is the writer trying to tell me?* If you can't answer these questions because you don't understand some of the words, then there are some essential words you need to look up in your dictionary.

Read the following sentences from "My Early Memories" which show you how this works. Suppose you don't know the underlined word or expression in each sentence. Read the question. If you can answer the question in italics, the word or expression is not essential. If you can't, it is essential.

1. I was born on April 5, 1937, at a time when my family was living on Morningside Avenue in <u>Harlem</u>.
   Question: *When and where was Powell born?*
   Reader's Thinking: I see his birth date and I suppose Harlem is where the Powells lived when Colin was born. It's probably the name of a place because it has a capital letter. That's all I need right now.

2. I have no <u>recollection</u> of the Harlem years.
   Question: *What is the writer telling me?*
   Reader's Thinking: I don't know so I guess the word could be important, but the sentence doesn't seem to tell me anything important about what's happening, so I'll keep on reading.

3. They say our earliest memories usually <u>involve a trauma</u>, and mine does.
   Question: *What's the writer telling me about early memories?*
   Reader's Thinking: These words are important, but maybe if I keep reading I'll understand them later.

4. I was four, and we had moved to the South Bronx. Gram Alice McKoy, my <u>maternal</u> grandmother, was taking care of me, since both my parents worked.
   Question: *Who took care of Powell while his parents worked?*
   Reader's Thinking: I don't know the word *maternal*, but *grandmother* is enough.

5. I was playing on the floor and <u>stuck a hairpin</u> into an <u>electrical outlet</u>. I remember the blinding <u>flash</u> and the <u>shock</u> almost <u>lifting</u> me off the floor.
   Question: *What happened? What did Colin do?*
   Reader's Thinking: These words are important because they tell me what Colin did. There are no definitions, so let me try using what's in the text. He was playing on the floor with a *hairpin*, with something used for the hair. Maybe something his grandmother uses in her hair. What words go with *outlet?*—an *electrical outlet.* That must be where you put the electrical cord. I think he put a hairpin where the electrical cord goes, so *stuck* means something like *put.* *Flash* and *shock* must be something to do with electricity. This event was bad, so I suppose *trauma* means something bad.

6. And I still remember Gram <u>scolding</u> and <u>hugging</u> me at the same time.
   Question: *What did Gram do?*
   Reader's Thinking: *Scolding* and *hugging*: these verbs are important. They tell me what Gram did. No definitions; I really can't guess exactly what she did. Let's see what the dictionary says.

scold /skoʊld/ v. [T] to tell someone in an angry way that s/he has done something wrong: *Mom **scolded** me for wasting electricity. –**scolding** n. [C,U]*

hug /hʌg/ v. **-gged, -gging** [T]. **1** to put your arms around someone and hold him/her tightly to show love or friendship **2** to move along the side, edge, top etc. of something, staying very close to it: *a boat hugging the coast*

Gram talked angrily to Colin, but at the same time she put her arms around him and held him tightly. That makes sense. She was angry at him, but she still loved him.

7. When my mother and father came home from work, much <u>intense</u> discussion occurred, followed by more scolding and <u>fussing</u>.
   Question: *What happened when Colin's parents came home?*
   Reader's Thinking: They talked, and scolded him more. I don't know what kind of discussion it was or what *fussing* means I don't need to know now.

8. My <u>keenest</u> memory of that day is not of the shock and pain, but of feeling important, being the center of attention, seeing how much they loved and cared about me.
   Question: *What does Powell remember about that day?*
   Reader's Thinking: He remembers being important, the center of attention, and loved. I think I can infer some meaning for *keenest*. It's the most something—maybe important, but it's not essential.

After You Read

For academic reading, you should do something to help you remember the ideas in what you read. For example, you might go back and mark important ideas with a highlighter. If one of your purposes is to learn more vocabulary, you should keep some kind of record of the new words and expressions that are important to you. We recommend making a vocabulary card, like the example below, for important words and multiword expressions. On the front, write the word and its part of speech (*noun, verb, adjective,* or *adverb*). On the back, write: 1) the context you read it in, 2) the definition, and, if it helps you, 3) the equivalent in your language. The most important of these three things is the context. You learn how to use words and expressions in English by noticing how English speakers and writers use them.

take care of v.	1) *"Gram . . . <u>was taking care of</u> me since both my parents worked."* *OR* *His grandmother <u>took care of</u> Powell while his parents were at work.* 2) *Watching and helping* 3) *[Equivalent in your language]*
FRONT OF CARD	BACK OF CARD

Other important words and expressions from this paragraph that you should make word cards for are: *involve a trauma, care for, hug,* and *scold.*

We hope this book helps you become a better reader with a larger vocabulary so that you can make the transition to authentic readings. We also hope you enjoy the selections we have chosen.

Growing Up

Discuss

1. What are some of the ingredients of a happy childhood?
2. What are some of the difficulties of growing up at different ages and in different family situations?

> *All my life I used to wonder what I would become when I grew up. Then about seven years ago, I realized that I never was going to grow up (that growing is an ever ongoing process).*
>
> M. Scott Peck, *Further Along the Road Not Traveled*

CHAPTER 1

ABOUT THE READING

This selection is from Colin L. Powell's autobiography, *My American Journey.* Powell's parents came to New York City from Jamaica, an island nation in the Caribbean. When Powell was young, he didn't seem to have any special talents or a clear idea of what he wanted in life. That changed in college when he chose a career in the army. He became a general and was the top military advisor to the forty-first president of the United States, George H. W. Bush, from 1988 to 1992. He served as secretary of state under the forty-third president of the United States, George W. Bush, from 2001 to 2004, retiring to private life at the end of Bush's first term.

BEFORE YOU READ

Thinking about the Topic

Discuss these questions.

1. What is your earliest memory from your childhood?
2. Why do you think you remember it clearly?

Previewing

You already read the title and paragraph 1 in the Introductory Chapter. Now read the first sentence of paragraphs 2–4. Complete the sentences below.

1. Based on the first sentence in paragraph 2, it is (clear / not clear) what the paragraph is about.
2. Paragraph 3 is about Powell's ability in _____.
3. Paragraph 4 begins talking about Powell's ability in _____.

Before you read, turn to Comprehension Check, First Reading, on page 4. Your purpose for the first reading is to be able to answer those questions.

My Early Memories *By Colin L. Powell*

1   I was born on April 5, 1937, at a time when my family was living on Morningside Avenue in Harlem. My parents' first child, my sister, Marilyn, had been born five and a half years before. I have no recollection of the Harlem years. They say our earliest memories usually involve a trauma, and mine does. I was four, and we had moved to the South Bronx. Gram Alice McKoy, my maternal grandmother, was taking care of me, since both my parents worked. I was playing on the floor and stuck a hairpin into an electrical outlet. I remember the blinding flash and the shock almost lifting me off the floor. And I still remember Gram scolding and hugging me at the same time. When my mother and father came home from work, much intense discussion occurred, followed by more scolding and fussing. My keenest memory of that day is not of the shock and pain, but of feeling important, being the center of attention, seeing how much they loved and cared about me.

2   When I was nine, catastrophe[1] struck the Powell family. As a student at P.S.[2] 39, I passed from the third to the fourth grade, but into the bottom form, called "Four Up," a euphemism meaning the kid is a little **slow**. This was the sort of secret to be whispered with shaking heads in our family circle. Education was the escape hatch, the way up and out for West Indians. My sister was already an excellent student, destined for college. And here I was, having difficulty in the fourth grade. I **lacked drive**, not ability. I was a happy-go-lucky kid, amenable,[3] amiable,[4] and aimless.

3   I was not much of an athlete either, though I enjoyed street games. One of my boyhood friends, Tony Grant, once counted thirty-six of them, stickball, stoopball, punchball, sluggo, and hot beans and butter among them. One day, I was playing baseball in an empty lot and saw my father coming down the street. I prayed he would keep on going, because I was having a bad day. But he stopped and watched. All the while Pop was there, I never connected. A swing and a miss, again and again, every time I was at bat. I can still feel the burning humiliation. It was always painful for me to disappoint my father. I imagined a pressure that probably was not there, since he rarely **uttered a word of reproach to me**.

4   As a boy, I took piano lessons; but the lessons did not take with me, and they soon ended. I later studied the flute. Marilyn thought the noises coming out of it were hilarious. I gave up the flute too. Apparently, I would not be a **jock** or a musician. Still, I was a contented kid, growing up in the warmth and security of the concentric circles[5] my family formed. At the center stood my parents. In the next circle were my mother's sisters and their families. My father's only sibling in America, Aunt Beryl, formed the next circle by herself. These circles rippled out[6] in diminishing degrees of **kinship**, but maintained considerable closeness. Family members looked out for, prodded,[7] and propped up[8] each other.

---

[1]**catastrophe** *something really terrible, probably an exaggeration for humor here*
[2]**P.S.** *public school*
[3]**amenable** *will listen to people, will do what people ask*
[4]**amiable** *friendly*
[5]**concentric circles** *(see picture at right)*
[6]**rippled out** *moved like water when you throw a stone in it*
[7]**prodded** *pushed, motivated*
[8]**propped up** *helped, supported*

slow
a. slow to learn
b. slow moving

lacked drive
a. took a trip in a car
b. didn't have the desire to succeed

uttered a word of reproach to me
a. thanked me
b. criticized me

jock
a. athlete
b. teacher

kinship
a. friendship
b. family relationship

COMPREHENSION CHECK

First Reading

Answer these questions.

1. What is Powell's first memory?
2. Does Powell say his childhood was happy or unhappy?
3. What, if anything, was Powell exceptionally good at when he was a boy?

Second Reading

Read the selection again. Match the beginning of each sentence on the left with the correct reason on the right to form a complete sentence.

_____ 1. Colin Powell got a shock, and Gram scolded him

_____ 2. Gram hugged him

_____ 3. Colin Powell passed to the low group in the fourth grade

_____ 4. Powell hoped his father wouldn't stop to watch him play baseball

_____ 5. Powell was basically a happy child

_____ 6. Education was especially important to Powell's family

a. because he wasn't particularly interested in school.

b. because he didn't want to look bad in front of his father and disappoint him.

c. because he put a metal hairpin in an electric outlet.

d. because he lived in a circle of relatives who loved and supported him.

e. because it was the way to a better life in their new country.

f. because she loved him and was worried about him.

VOCABULARY

Vocabulary Building

Read the underlined word or expression in its context and match it with the correct meaning. The paragraph number is in parentheses. Use a dictionary if necessary.

PART 1

____ 1. I was a happy-go-lucky kid, amenable, amiable, and <u>aimless</u>. (¶2)

____ 2. I <u>prayed</u> he would keep on going. . . . (¶3)

____ 3. I can still feel burning <u>humiliation</u>. (¶3)

____ 4. It was always painful for me to <u>disappoint</u> my father. (¶3)

____ 5. I imagined a <u>pressure</u> that probably was not there. . . . (¶3)

____ 6. Marilyn thought the noises coming out of (the flute) were <u>hilarious</u>. (¶4)

a. the force of someone pushing you, trying to influence you

b. hoped very much, wanted strongly

c. very funny

d. without a clear purpose or direction

e. feeling of shame or embarrassment

f. make someone unhappy because something is not as good as expected

PART 2

____ 7. I <u>gave up</u> the flute too. (¶4)

____ 8. <u>Apparently</u>, I would not be a jock or a musician. (¶4)

____ 9. Still, I was a <u>contented</u> kid. . . . (¶4)

____10. These circles rippled out in <u>diminishing</u> degrees of kinship. . . . (¶4)

____11. . . . but <u>maintained</u> considerable closeness. (¶4)

____12. Family members <u>looked out for</u> . . . each other. (¶4)

g. continued, kept up

h. protected, kept safe

i. happy

j. stopped, quit

k. it seems

l. getting smaller

Handling Non-essential Vocabulary

Read each sentence and skip the crossed-out words. Demonstrate that the word or words are not essential by answering the questions. Even though the words are not essential, you can infer partial meaning. Circle the choice for the partial meaning that makes sense in the context. If you are curious about the words, look them up in your dictionary.

PARAGRAPH 2

1. As a student at P.S. 39, I passed from the third to the fourth grade, but into the bottom form, called "Four Up," ~~a euphemism~~ meaning the kid is a little slow.

   Was Powell one of the best students in the fourth grade? _____

   Euphemism is probably   a. a polite way of saying something.   b. a school subject.

2. This was the sort of secret to be ~~whispered~~ with shaking heads in our family circle.

   Did Powell's family feel good or bad that he was in "Four Up"? _____

   Whispered is probably   a. a way of talking.   b. a way of moving.

3. Education was the escape ~~hatch~~, the way up and out for West Indians.

   Why was doing well in school important for West Indians? _____

   _____

   Hatch is probably   a. a chicken egg.   b. an opening, a doorway.

4. My sister was already an excellent student, ~~destined~~ for college.

   Was Marilyn a good student or not?   _____

   In this sentence *destined* probably means

   a. sure (to go to college).   b. not sure (to go to college).

PARAGRAPH 4

5. As a boy, I took piano lessons; but the lessons ~~did not take with me~~, and they soon ended.

   Did Powell do well in his piano lessons?   _____

   The lessons *did not take with me* probably means

   a. he liked the lessons.   b. he didn't like the lessons.

6. Still, I was a contented kid, growing up in the warmth and ~~security~~ of the concentric circles my family formed.

   Were relationships in the Powell family good or bad? _____

   Security probably means   a. safety.   b. difficulty.

7. These circles rippled out in diminishing degrees of kinship, but maintained ~~considerable~~ closeness.

   Did Powell's relatives stay fairly close, or were they distant from each other? _____

   Considerable probably means   a. no.   b. quite a bit of.

Vocabulary Review

Complete the following statements about the reading selection with the correct word or expression from the list below. Use each word or expression only once.

disappoint	hugged	looked out for
gave up	involved a trauma	scolded
hilarious	lacked drive	

1. Colin Powell's first memory _____. He stuck a hairpin in an electric outlet and got a big shock.

2. Even though his grandmother got angry and _____ him, what he remembers most is that she _____ him because she loved and cared about him.

3. Powell wasn't an excellent student; he wasn't stupid, but he

   _____.

4. Powell enjoyed games, but he wasn't a very good athlete. Once when he was playing baseball, his father stopped to watch. He didn't want to

   _____ his father, but he never hit the ball.

5. He took flute lessons, too. His sister thought the sounds that came out of his flute were _____. Since he lacked musical ability, he

   _____ the flute.

6. Powell wasn't a star early in life; however, the security of his early life among relatives who loved and _____ him gave him a strong foundation for later success.

TEXT ANALYSIS *Narrative Writing*

Narrative writing is used to tell a story or to describe events or incidents. When writers tell about incidents, they usually answer most of these questions:

1. Where did the incident happen?
2. When did it happen?
3. Who was there?
4. What happened? What did people do? Why?
5. How did the people feel? Why?

Remember to use these question words (*where, when, who, what, how*) when you think about what to include in a narrative.

Work with a partner. Read paragraphs 1 and 3 again. Tell or narrate the incidents in these paragraphs in your own words using the questions in the box on page 7 as a guide. You may want to answer the questions in a different order. Make a written copy of your narration.

Example beginning for paragraph 1:

One day, when Colin Powell was four years old, his grandmother was taking care of him.   (Answers questions 2 and 3.)

Continue your narration with the answers to questions 1, 4, and 5.

RESPONDING TO READING

Discuss these questions.

1. In discussing the questions on the introductory page, you talked about the ingredients of a happy childhood. Which of the things you mentioned were part of Powell's childhood?

2. What is important to the different members of the Powell family? Do you think that any of these things are more important to immigrant families than to other families?

3. What, if any, pressure did Powell's family put on him when he was young? How can parental expectations put both positive and negative pressure on children?

"Peer Influences on Achievement" comes from the book *Beyond the Classroom* (1996) by Laurence Steinberg, a professor of psychology at Temple University in Philadelphia. The book is about research he did with Bradford Brown from the University of Wisconsin and Sanford M. Dornbusch from Stanford University. They studied American adolescents over a ten-year period. They collected information from more than 20,000 teenagers from nine high schools and spoke with many of their parents and teachers.

BEFORE YOU READ

Thinking about the Topic

People in our lives put *pressure* on us. They try to *influence* (affect) our *behavior* (actions), our thinking, and our decisions. We seem to feel and react to this pressure most during *adolescence* (the period between childhood and adulthood).

Look at the chart below. List three examples of pressure or influence that young people experience. Then list the source of that pressure or influence. How do young people often react to each one?

Example	Source of Pressure
pressure not to use bad words	*my mother, in particular*

Previewing

The title of this selection contains difficult words. Read their dictionary entries below and then answer the questions that follow.

> **peer** /pɪər/ *n.* someone who is the same age as you
>
> **in·flu·ence** /ˈɪnfluəns/ *n.* someone or something that has an effect on other people or things
>
> **a·chieve·ment** /əˈtʃivmənt/ *n.* success in doing or getting what you worked for

1. What do you think this selection is about?

   a. the effect of parents on schoolwork

   b. the effect of friends on schoolwork

2. This selection comes from a book that reports on a long-term research project. Knowing this, what do you think was the writer's general purpose for writing the book?

   a. to give facts about peer pressure on teenagers

   b. to give opinions about peer pressure on teenagers

Before you read, turn to Comprehension Check, First Reading, on page 11. Your purpose for the first reading is to be able to answer those questions.

READ

tracking
a. following
b. running

whether
a. because
b. if

actually
a. really
b. acting

aspirations
a. plans
b. memories

concerned about
a. uninterested in
b. worried about

Peer Influences on Achievement
By Laurence Steinberg

1   By **tracking** students over a three-year period, we were able to see how they were doing in school at the beginning of the time period, which friends they were spending time with, and **whether** their school performance and behavior changed over time as a result. By comparing the academic careers of students who began high school with equivalent grades, but who had different sorts of friends during the school years, we were able to see whether the type of friends that adolescents have **actually** makes a difference in their school performance.

2   The answer is that it most certainly does, especially in two areas: academic performance and delinquency. Youngsters whose friends were more academically oriented—that is, whose friends had higher grades, spent more time on homework, had higher educational **aspirations**, and who were more involved in extracurricular activities[1]—did better over the course of high school than students who began school with similar records but who had less academically oriented friends. Similarly, students whose friends were more delinquent—who used more drugs and alcohol and who had more conduct problems—developed more problems themselves over time than did adolescents who began the study with the same behavior profile but who had friends who were less delinquent.

3   These findings tell us, then, that parents have legitimate reason to be **concerned about** the qualities and values of their children's friends, especially during early adolescence, when susceptibility to peer influence runs strong.[2] There is also reason to be concerned about the characteristics of the crowd to which an adolescent belongs, since our study found that this influence matters, too. All other things being equal, adolescents who are members of more academically oriented crowds do better in school than other students, whereas those who are members of more alienated crowds do worse and are more likely to get into trouble.

4   How large a difference do friends make? In one set of analyses, we were able to contrast the influence of best friends with the influence of parents in two important areas: the grades in school that the adolescent was getting and the adolescent's amount of drug and alcohol use. At least by high school, the influence of friends on school performance and drug use is more substantial than the influence of parents' practices at home. Parents may influence their children's long-term educational plans, but when it comes to day-to-day influences on schooling—whether students attend class, how much time they spend on homework, how hard they try in school, and the grades they bring home—friends are more influential than parents.

---

[1]**extracurricular activities** *activities outside classes (sports, music groups, clubs)*
[2]**when susceptibility to peer influence runs strong** *when the person is easily influenced by peers*

COMPREHENSION CHECK

First Reading

Answer these questions.

1. According to this study, who has the most influence on the schoolwork of American high school students: their parents, their friends, or their teachers?
2. In what areas is the influence of these people greatest?

Second Reading

A. Read the selection again. Mark the statements *T* (true) or *F* (false). Write the paragraph number(s) where you found evidence for each answer.

DESIGN OF THE STUDY

1. T F The researchers compared groups of students who had similar grades but different kinds of friends at the beginning of high school.   ¶ ____

2. T F They compared the students' grades at the beginning of the school year with their grades at the end of the year.   ¶ ____

FINDINGS OF THE STUDY

3. T F Students who had academically oriented friends had better grades over the course of high school.   ¶ ____

4. T F Students who had less academically oriented friends had worse grades and were less likely to use drugs and alcohol.   ¶ ____

5. T F Close friends and crowds both had an important influence on students' grades and behavior.   ¶ ____

B. Complete the sentences with information from paragraph 4.

1. Parents may influence _____.

2. Friends influence _____.

Vocabulary Building

Read the underlined word or expression in its context and match it with the correct meaning. The paragraph number is in parentheses. Use a dictionary if necessary.

___ 1. By comparing the <u>academic careers</u> of students . . . (¶1)

___ 2. . . . students who began high school with <u>equivalent</u> grades, but who had different sorts of friends . . . (¶1)

___ 3. . . . especially in two areas: academic performance and <u>delinquency</u>. (¶2)

___ 4. Youngsters whose friends were more <u>academically oriented</u> . . . (¶2)

___ 5. . . . students . . . who had more <u>conduct</u> problems . . . (¶2)

___ 6. These <u>findings</u> tell us . . . that parents have . . . reason to be concerned. . . . (¶3)

___ 7. . . . the characteristics of the <u>crowd</u> . . . (¶3)

___ 8. . . . those who are members of more <u>alienated</u> crowds do worse. . . . (¶3)

___ 9. In one set of <u>analyses</u>, . . . (¶4)

___10. . . . we were able to <u>contrast</u> the influence of best friends with the influence of parents. . . . (¶4)

a. careful examination of data or information

b. feeling separated from those around you

c. research results, information someone has learned from a study

d. the way someone acts, behavior

e. all aspects of school years (in this case, grades and behavior)

f. show differences

g. equal in value

h. group with common interests

i. interested in school

j. illegal or socially unacceptable behavior

Identifying Essential and Non-essential Vocabulary

Read the sentences and skip the underlined words. Decide which words or phrases are essential and which are not essential. Write *E* for essential and *NE* for non-essential.

1. (¶1) We were able to see <u>how they (students) were doing</u> at the beginning of the time <u>period</u>.

   a. (how they were doing) ___*E*___   b. (period) ___*NE*___

2. (¶1) By comparing the academic careers of students who began high school with <u>equivalent</u> grades, but who had different <u>sorts of</u> friends during the school years, we were able to see whether the type of friends that adolescents have actually makes a difference in their school performance.

   a. (equivalent) _____   b. (sorts of) _____

3. (¶2) Similarly, students whose friends were more delinquent . . . developed more problems themselves over time than did adolescents who began the study with the same <u>behavior</u> <u>profile</u> but who had friends who were less delinquent.

    a. (behavior) _____   b. (profile) _____

4. (¶3) These findings tell us, then, that parents have <u>legitimate</u> reason to be <u>concerned</u> about the qualities and values of their children's friends. . . .

    a. (legitimate) _____   b. (concerned) _____

Vocabulary Review

Complete the following statements about the reading selection with the correct word or expression from the list below. Use each word or expression only once.

academically oriented	conduct	peers
achievement	crowds	whether
concerned	findings	

1. The researchers who did this study wanted to know _____ parents or friends had a greater influence on the academic performance and behavior of adolescents.

2. The _____ of the study show that friends are more influential than parents in two areas: grades and _____.

3. Parents should be _____ about their children's friends because youngsters who have more _____ friends do better in school. Their academic _____ is higher.

4. All other things being equal, students in more alienated _____ do worse academically.

5. This research showed the importance of _____ in young people's lives.

TEXT ANALYSIS

Topic and Main Idea

> **Topic:** Every piece of writing—a book, a newspaper article, even a paragraph—is about something, which is the *topic* of the writing. Topics can be general (for example, *The Internet* or *The environment*) or more specific (for example, *Identity theft on the Internet* or *The melting of the polar ice caps and the threat to polar bears*).
>
> **Main Idea:** Every piece of writing expresses several ideas about the topic, but there is usually one general, central idea that is called the *main idea*. If an idea is too general or too specific, it is not the best expression of the main idea. A main idea is always expressed as a complete sentence.

Work with a partner. Answer these questions.

1. Which is the best topic for this selection?
    a. parental pressure to get good grades
    b. influence of peers on academic work and behavior
    c. research results in American schools
2. Which is the best main idea for the selection?
    a. Students in American schools don't value academic achievement, and they often abuse alcohol and drugs.
    b. Parents should help their children choose their friends and stop them from using drugs and drinking alcohol.
    c. Research shows that during high school, friends have a greater effect than parents on an adolescent's grades and use of alcohol and drugs.

Finding the Writer's Definition

When writers have a specific meaning for a word or expression, they often include the definition between dashes (— . . . —). Refer to the indicated paragraph, and copy the author's definition. The first one has been started for you.

1. (¶2) By *academically oriented*, the writer means **_a student whose friends_**
   _____ .

2. (¶2) By *delinquent*, the writer means _____
   _____ .

3. (¶4) By *day-to-day influences on schooling*, the writer means _____
   _____ .

RESPONDING TO READING

Discuss these questions.

1. On the basis of the findings in this study, Steinberg comments that parents should be concerned about the friends their children choose. What, if anything, do you think parents can do to help their children choose the right friends?

2. There are a lot of influences on young people in today's world. Some are listed here. Add others you think of.

   parents
   close friends
   the Internet
   advertising
   others: _____

3. Who or what influences young people in the following areas? Give specific examples of their influence based on your experience.
    a. choice of friends
    b. the amount of studying done
    c. free-time activities
    d. music preferences
    e. part-time employment
    f. dangerous behaviors
    g. career choice

CHAPTER 3

ABOUT THE READING

"It's OK to Be Different" appeared in *Newsweek*, October 24, 1994, when Angie Erickson was in ninth grade. She has since graduated from the University of Minnesota with a degree in family social science. She wanted a job where she could help other people. Although it wasn't easy to find a job because of her disability, she was finally hired by Opportunity Partners, an organization that helps people with developmental disabilities to achieve their dreams through employment and life skills. She is a service planner who helps clients to find and retain employment. She says, "By far the best part of my day is when I can see my clients overcoming the barriers put in front of them."

BEFORE YOU READ

Thinking about the Topic

Discuss these questions.

1. What is a disability? List some disabilities you know of.
2. In your experience, how do people of various ages treat people with disabilities?

Previewing

Read the title, the subtitle, and the first two paragraphs of this selection, and answer the questions.

1. What is Angie's disability?
2. What problems did she face?

Before you read, turn to Comprehension Check, First Reading, on page 17. Your purpose for the first reading is to be able to answer those questions.

READ

It's OK to Be Different

Stop Making Fun of My Disability   *By Angie Erickson*

1   Why me? I often ask myself. Why did I have to be the one? Why did I get picked to be different? Why are people mean to me and always treating me differently? These are the kinds of questions that I used to ask myself. It took more than ten years for me to find answers and to realize that I'm not more different than anyone else.

2   I was born on June 29, 1978. Along with me came my twin sister, Stephanie. She was born with no birth defects,[1] but I was born with cerebral palsy.[2] For me, CP made it so I shake a little; when my sister began to walk, I couldn't. The doctors knew it was a minor case of cerebral palsy. But they didn't know if I'd ever walk straight or do things that other kids my age could do.

---

[1]**birth defects** *abnormalities present at birth that affect the structure or function of the body*
[2]**cerebral palsy (CP)** *an illness caused by damage to a baby's brain before it is born, which makes muscles permanently weak*

blame myself
a. say I was happy
b. say I was responsible

teased
a. laughed at
b. helped

ignore
a. pay attention to
b. not pay attention to

willpower
a. determination and strength
b. muscle power

3   At first my disability did not bother me, because when you're a toddler, you do things that are really easy. When it took me a little longer to play yard games, because I couldn't run that well, my friends just thought I was slow. My disability was noticed when other children were learning how to write and I couldn't. Kids I thought were my friends started to stay away from me because they said I was different. Classmates began commenting on my speech. They said I talked really weird. Every time someone was mean to me, I would start to cry and I would always **blame myself** for being different.

4   People thought I was stupid because it was hard for me to write my own name. So when I was the only one in the class to use a typewriter,[3] I began to feel I was different. It got worse when the third graders moved on to fourth grade and I had to stay behind. I got held back because the teachers thought I'd be unable to type fast enough to keep up. Kids told me that was a lie and the reason I got held back was because I was a retard.[4] It really hurt to be **teased** by those I thought were my friends.

5   After putting up with everyone making fun of me and me crying about it, I started sticking up for myself when I was ten, in fourth grade. I realized if I wanted them to stop, I would have to be the person who made them stop. I finally found out who my real friends were, and I tried to **ignore** the ones who were mean. Instead of constantly thinking about the things I couldn't do, I tried to think about the things I could do, and it helped others, and myself, understand who I really was. When there was something I couldn't do, such as play Pictionary, I sat and I watched or I would go find something else to do. A few people still called me names and made fun of me, but after a while, when they saw they didn't get a reaction, they quit, because it wasn't fun anymore. What they didn't know was that it did still hurt me. It hurt me a lot more than they could ever imagine.

6   It took a lot of **willpower** on my part and a lot of love from family and friends to get where I am today. I learned that no one was to blame for my disability. I realize that I can do things and I can do them very well. Some things I can't do, like taking my own notes in class or running in a race, but I will have to live with that. At sixteen, I believe I've learned more than many people will learn in their whole lives. I have worked out that some people are just mean because they're afraid of being nice. They try to prove to themselves and others that they are cool,[5] but, sooner or later, they're going to wish they hadn't said some of those hurtful things. A lot of people will go through life being mean to those with disabilities because they don't know how to act or what to say to them—they feel awkward with someone who's different.

7   Parents need to teach their children that it's all right to be different and it's all right to be friends with those who are. Some think that the disabled should be treated like little kids for the rest of their lives. They presume we don't need love and friends, but our needs are the same as every other human being's.

8   There are times when I wish I hadn't been born with cerebral palsy, but crying about it isn't going to do me any good. I can only live once, so I want to live the best I can. I am glad I learned who I am and what I am capable of doing. I am happy with who I am. Nobody else could be the Angela Marie Erickson who is writing this. I could never be, or ever want to be, anyone else.

---

[3]**typewriter** *(see picture at right)*
[4]**retard** *a stupid person (slang, offensive, comes from the outdated term mentally retarded)*
[5]**cool** *someone or something that is fashionable, attractive, or relaxed (informal, spoken)*

First Reading

Answer these questions.

1. How did Angie's disability affect her mental and physical abilities?
2. How did it affect her friendships?

Second Reading

A. Read the selection again. Mark the statements *T* (true) or *F* (false). Write the paragraph number(s) where you found evidence for each answer.

1. T F Angie had a serious case of cerebral palsy. ¶ ___

2. T F Her disability first became a real problem for her in school. ¶ ___

3. T F She didn't pass to the fourth grade because she wasn't smart enough. ¶ ___

4. T F Angie learned that if she didn't react, kids stopped making fun of her. ¶ ___

5. T F According to Angie, one reason people are mean to others with disabilities is that they don't feel comfortable with someone who is different. ¶ ___

6. T F Angie thinks disabled people have different emotional needs from other people. ¶ ___

B. For each item below, check (✓) the results. Be prepared to show evidence from the selection for the results you check.

1. Angie had a mild case of CP. As a result, she

   ☐ a. shook a little.

   ☐ b. started walking late.

   ☐ c. couldn't walk or run very well.

   ☐ d. couldn't write.

   ☐ e. couldn't talk at all.

2. Kids teased and made fun of Angie. As a result, she

   ☐ a. talked to the teacher about them.

   ☐ b. cried.

   ☐ c. felt hurt.

   ☐ d. blamed herself for her problems.

3. Angie was the only child to use a typewriter, so she

   ☐ a. felt different.

   ☐ b. was held back in the third grade.

   ☐ c. could write faster on her typewriter.

4. Angie's life was not easy. As a result, she learned things. The difficulties taught her

☐ a. that to stop the teasing she had to ignore it.

☐ b. that she could do anything she wanted.

☐ c. who her real friends were.

☐ d. that she should focus on what she could do and not on what she couldn't do.

C. Circle the letter of the topic and main idea of this selection.

1. Topic

   a. American schools

   b. mean kids

   c. living with a disability

2. Main idea

   a. People with disabilities should always ask for help because they can't do everything by themselves.

   b. Angie learned to accept herself and learned to live with being different.

   c. Kids can be cruel to others without knowing they are hurting them.

VOCABULARY

Vocabulary Building

SYNONYMS
It is a generally accepted rule of good writing not to repeat words or expressions too often. Therefore writers use synonyms—words or phrases with the same or almost the same meaning—to add variety to their writing. Knowing sets of synonyms increases your vocabulary to make you both a better reader and a better writer.

Read the underlined word or expression in its context. Circle the two choices that are similar in meaning in this context. Use a dictionary if necessary.

1. Why are people <u>mean</u> to me and always treating me differently? (¶1)

   a. nice   b. cruel   c. unkind

2. The doctors knew it was a <u>minor</u> case of cerebral palsy. (¶2)

   a. not serious   b. not very important   c. serious

3. At first my disability did not <u>bother</u> me, . . . (¶3)

   a. upset   b. disturb   c. help

4. . . . when you're a <u>toddler</u>, you do things that are really easy. (¶3)

   a. little kid   b. teenager   c. preschooler

5. Classmates began <u>commenting on</u> my speech. (¶3)

   a. talking about   b. planning   c. mentioning

6. They said I talked really <u>weird</u>. (¶3)

    a. too fast   b. in a strange way   c. in an odd way

7. . . . they feel <u>awkward</u> with someone who's different. (¶6)

    a. embarrassed   b. relaxed   c. uncomfortable

8. They <u>presume</u> we don't need love and friends. . . . (¶7)

    a. remember   b. suppose   c. think

9. . . . what I <u>am capable of doing</u>. (¶8)

    a. can do   b. am able to do   c. try to do

Multiword Expressions

Read the underlined multiword expression in its context. Choose the meaning that makes sense in this context. Use a dictionary if necessary.

1. Stop <u>making fun of</u> my disability.

    a. enjoying   b. laughing at   c. talking about

2. Kids . . . started to <u>stay away from</u> me because they said I was different. (¶3)

    a. give help to   b. keep a distance from   c. visit

3. . . . when the third graders moved on . . . I had to <u>stay behind</u>. (¶4)

    a. get help   b. leave school   c. repeat the grade

4. I <u>got held back</u> because the teachers thought I'd be unable to type fast enough. . . . (¶4)

    a. didn't pass to the next grade

    b. passed to the next grade

    c. was expelled from school

5. . . . the teachers thought I'd be unable to type fast enough to <u>keep up</u>. (¶4)

    a. continue working

    b. hold something up

    c. work as fast as the other students

6. After <u>putting up with</u> everyone making fun of me . . . (¶5)

    a. choosing   b. liking   c. tolerating

7. . . . I started <u>sticking up for</u> myself. . . . (¶5)

    a. defending   b. escaping   c. forgetting

8. I finally <u>found out</u> who my real friends were. . . . (¶5)

    a. looked for   b. learned, discovered   c. thought about

Vocabulary Review

Complete the following statements about the reading selection with the correct word or expression from the list below. Use each word or expression only once.

awkward	keep up	tease
blamed	mean	weird
capable	minor	willpower
ignore	stay behind	

1. Angie had a(n) _____ case of cerebral palsy, so there were some things she couldn't do.

2. Kids who didn't understand her disability were _____ to her; they called her names and made fun of her.

3. Teachers didn't help the situation when they said she had to _____ in third grade. They thought she couldn't type fast enough to _____ with the other children.

4. For a long time, Angie _____ herself for being different.

5. When she was in the fourth grade, she finally realized that many people feel _____ with someone who is different.

6. Angie learned to _____ the kids who said that she talked _____.

7. Angie learned another important thing. People who _____ others are trying to get a reaction, and when they don't get it, they stop.

8. It took a lot of _____ on her part and love from her family for Angie to focus on the things she is _____ of doing rather than the things she can't do.

TEXT ANALYSIS

Paragraph Topics

This selection follows a common type of organization: Introduction, Body, and Conclusion. Match each paragraph in the body with its topic.

¶1 Introduction
¶2 ____
¶3 ____
¶4 ____
¶5 ____
¶6 ____
¶7 ____
¶8 Conclusion

a. how Angie's thinking and behavior change

b. early years and the beginning of problems

c. what Angie learned

d. conditions of Angie's birth

e. Angie's comments for parents

f. people's reactions to Angie

RESPONDING TO READING

Discuss these questions.

1. What do you think is the most important thing Angie learned? Why do you consider it important?

2. Would Angie get the same reactions from children in your culture? Why or why not?

3. Talk about people you know who have grown up with a disability or are different from other people in some way. How have they handled their situation? What kind of people are they?

"To a Daughter Leaving Home" was published in 1988 in a collection of poems called *The Imperfect Paradise.* Linda Pastan (1932–) is a contemporary American poet who typically writes short poems about topics such as family life, the female experience, fear of loss, and death.

BEFORE YOU READ

Thinking about the Topic

Discuss these questions and fill in the chart below.

1. How do you think parents feel as they watch their children grow up? Write additional adjectives in the chart below.
2. In the second column, fill in when parents might feel this way.

How Parents Feel	When
proud	when children graduate from school
worried	

Before you read, turn to Comprehension Check, First Reading on page 23. Your purpose for the first reading is to be able to answer those questions.

READ

To a Daughter Leaving Home

By Linda Pastan

1   When I taught you
at eight to ride
a bicycle, loping[1] along
beside you

5   as you wobbled[2] away
on two round wheels,
my own mouth rounding
in surprise when you pulled
ahead down the curved

---

[1]**loping** *running easily using long steps*
[2]**wobbled** *moved from side to side in an unsteady way*

10   path of the park,
         I kept waiting
         for the thud[3]
         of your crash as I
         sprinted[4] to catch up,

15   while you grew
         smaller, more breakable
         with distance,
         pumping, pumping[5]
         for your life, screaming

20   with laughter,
         the hair flapping[6]
         behind you like a
         handkerchief waving
         goodbye.

---

[3]**thud** *the low sound that is made by something heavy hitting something else*
[4]**sprinted** *ran very fast for a short distance*
[5]**pumping** *moving the legs quickly up and down*
[6]**flapping** *moving in the wind*

COMPREHENSION CHECK

First Reading

Answer these questions.

1. How old was the daughter when this incident happened?
2. What were the daughter and parent doing?

Second Reading

Read the poem at least one more time. Then answer the questions. Write the line number(s) where you found evidence for each answer. Compare your answers with your classmates.

1. Why is the parent surprised by the daughter? _____
   _____ **Line(s)** _____

2. What does the parent expect? _____
   _____ **Line(s)** _____

3. How do you know the parent can't catch up? _____
   _____ **Line(s)** _____

4. How does the daughter feel? How do you know she feels that way? _____
   _____ **Line(s)** _____

5. How does the daughter look to the parent? _____
   _____ **Line(s)** _____

6. On a separate piece of paper, draw a picture of the scene described in this poem.

Images

Poets use words to create images that appeal to a reader's senses—to sight, hearing, smell, taste, and touch. To do this the poet often uses descriptive words, such as the word *loping*, which is a special type of running with long, easy steps.

Example: We can see the parent *loping* along beside the girl on the bike and not wanting to let go.

Simile and Metaphor

Writers of all kinds, poets and nonpoets, create images based on comparisons. If the comparison uses the word *like* or *as*, it is called a *simile*.

Example:

the hair flapping
behind you like a
handkerchief waving
goodbye.

If it does not use the word *like* or *as*, it is called a *metaphor*. Many everyday expressions are, in fact, metaphors.

Examples:

The arms and legs of the chair   The head and foot of the bed

Answer and complete the items below.

1. What other visual (sight) images and hearing (sound) images can you find in the poem? Look for descriptive vocabulary like *loping* that creates such images.

2. This whole poem is a metaphor. It compares _____

   to _____.

Discuss these questions.

1. How are leaving home and learning to ride a bicycle similar? Consider both the child's and the parent's point of view.

2. What does this poem suggest parents must do to help their children grow up? Is this easy or hard for parents to do? Explain.

3. What are some steps to growing up in your culture? Could any of those steps be a metaphor for all of growing up?

Extending Your Vocabulary

Word Families

One way to increase your vocabulary is to learn other forms of words you already know. Study the chart below to learn other forms of some of the words in this unit. If there is a box with a dash, either there is no word to fill it or the word is missing because it is not one you need to know now.

	NOUNS	VERBS	ADJECTIVES	ADVERBS
1.	academy	—	academic	academically
2.	achievement	achieve	—	—
3.	alien alienation	alienate	alienated	—
4.	analysis analyses (*pl.*)	analyze	analytical	analytically
5.	appearance	appear	apparent	apparently
6.	delinquency	—	delinquent	—
7.	disappointment	disappoint	disappointed disappointing	—
8.	humiliation	humiliate	humiliated humiliating	—
9.	influence	influence	influential	—
10.	trauma	traumatize	traumatic	—

For each item below, look at the row in the chart above with the same number. Choose the word that correctly completes the sentence. Be sure to use the correct form.

1. A school is sometimes called an _____.

2. People who work hard usually _____ more than lazy people.

3. I was careful in choosing my words. I didn't want to _____ anyone.

4. I have to _____ all the possibilities before I decide what to do. Fortunately, I have a(n) _____ mind.

5. Driving over the speed limit was the _____ cause of the accident.

6. The illegal behavior of young people is sometimes called juvenile

   _____.

(continued)

7. I was _____ when I did not get the job. It was awful to get _____ results from several companies.

8. It can be _____ to be criticized in public. I was _____ when my teacher criticized me in front of the class.

9. Senator Morales is a very _____ person; other people pay attention to what she says.

10. The accident _____ me. Now I'm afraid to drive.

Words with More Than One Meaning

In all languages, some words have more than one meaning, so another way to increase your vocabulary is to learn additional meanings for words. Read each sentence. Match the underlined word or expression with the correct meaning. In some cases, you will use the same answer twice, and there may be more than one correct answer. An asterisk indicates a meaning that was used in this unit.

1. ____ . . . they feel <u>awkward</u>* with someone who's different.

____ The young girl walked <u>awkwardly</u> in high-heeled shoes.

____ A bass guitar is a bit <u>awkward</u> to carry.

____ I caught my friend in a lie; it was a very <u>awkward</u> situation.

    a. uncomfortable

    b. difficult to use or handle

    c. moving or behaving in a way that does not seem relaxed or comfortable

2. ____ . . . parents have legitimate reason to be <u>concerned about</u>* the qualities and values of their children's friends.

____ They are only <u>concerned with</u> making money.

____ <u>As far as I'm concerned</u>, La Trattoria is the best restaurant in town.

____ Sorry, but this matter doesn't <u>concern</u> you.

    a. worried

    b. interested in

    c. involve, affect

    d. according to someone's opinion

3. ____ They say our earliest memories usually <u>involve</u>* a trauma. . . .

____ Some parents are so <u>involved in</u> their work, they don't have much time for their children.

____ This job <u>involves</u> a lot of travel.

____ We need to <u>involve</u> students in the discussion.

    a. include

    b. requires

    c. dedicated to

4. ___ Family members <u>look out for</u>*... each other.

___ The guards <u>look out for</u> strangers and report them.

___ <u>Look out</u>! There's a car coming fast.

a. protect, take care of

b. pay attention

c. watch for

5. ___ The doctors knew it was a <u>minor</u>* case of cerebral palsy.

___ There are many things that a <u>minor</u> can't buy in the United States.

___ I'm majoring in math with a <u>minor</u> in economics.

a. someone not old enough to be legally responsible

b. second main subject you study in college

c. not very important or serious

WRITING

Choose one of the suggestions for writing below. Talk about what you plan to write with a classmate who chose the same topic. Then follow the instructions for writing. Ask yourself *wh-* questions (*who, what, when, where, why, how*) to plan what you are going to say.

1. Growing up means becoming increasingly independent. Write about an important step toward independence in your life, such as getting your driver's license, getting your first job, or taking a trip for the first time without your parents.

2. Choose a person who has had a great influence on your life. Write about the person and the influence he or she has had.

3. Write about a difficulty you or someone you know had while growing up.

4. Peer influence is not the only influence on children growing up. Write about a celebrity you admire or do not admire for his or her influence on young people.

Try to use some of the following vocabulary in writing about the topic you choose: *awkward, behavior, bother, capable, crowd, disappoint, extracurricular activities, find out, give up, hug, involve, look out for, make fun of, mean, put pressure on, put up with, scold, stay away from, stick up for, tease, trauma, willpower.*

Between Two Worlds

Discuss

1. Why do people *emigrate*, or leave their country of origin to live in another country?
2. What are some of the changes in their lives that result from emigration?
3. What contributions do people make to the countries they emigrate to, or *host countries*? What contributions can they make to their *homeland*, or country of origin?

Between these two worlds
I am happy, confused, angry
And in pain—all at the same time.
For I am a door
Caught between two rooms.
I see and feel both of them
But I don't seem to belong to either.

Nagesh Rao, excerpt from "I am a door"

ABOUT THE READING

"People on the Move" is an excerpt from the introduction to *Moving Young*, the youth supplement to the UNFPA (United Nations Population Fund) report, *State of World Population 2006*.

BEFORE YOU READ

Thinking about the Topic

Discuss these questions.

1. Why have families you know emigrated from their homeland to another country?
2. Do families generally emigrate together or not? Why?
3. What areas of the world do people often emigrate from? What countries do they go to?

Previewing

Study the graphs below and the statistics on page 30. Answer the questions.

1. What regions of the world receive more people than they send?
2. What regions send more people than they receive?
3. As of 2005, how many people were living outside their country of birth?
4. How has the amount of international migration (moving from one country to another) changed since 1960? Talk about the changes in numbers over the years.
5. Look at the title of the article. What do you think it will focus on?

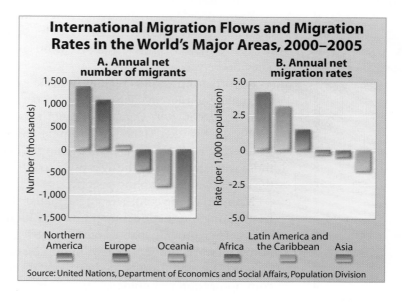

International Migration Flows and Migration Rates in the World's Major Areas, 2000–2005

A. Annual net number of migrants

Number (thousands)

1,500
1,000
500
0
-500
-1,000
-1,500

B. Annual net migration rates

Rate (per 1,000 population)

5.0
2.5
0
-2.5
-5.0

Northern America Europe Oceania Africa Latin America and the Caribbean Asia

Source: United Nations, Department of Economics and Social Affairs, Population Division

Before you read, turn to Comprehension Check, First Reading, on page 31. Your purpose for the first reading is to be able to answer those questions.

READ

People on the Move: Moving Young

better-off
a. poorer
b. richer

destination
a. where they are going
b. what they are studying

precarious
a. dangerous
b. safe

1   It is estimated that in 2005 there were over 191 million international migrants worldwide. The dream of better opportunities and demand for labor from abroad sets many young people in motion. Violence, war, poverty, unemployment, crime or persecution drive many others to escape.

2   A majority of young international migrants come from developing countries.[1] They emigrate to **better-off** neighboring countries or to developed countries.[2] Many leave with few belongings, little money and little information about their **destination**; but they take with them the great assets of youth: resilience, resourcefulness and perseverance. But, because of their age, they face obstacles and risks that test their endurance.

3   Young people on the move are determined. Many lack working papers and cross borders as visitors or tourists. Others pay smugglers to get them in. If necessary, they cross oceans in **precarious** boats or burning deserts hidden in cars. They find a way.

4   Reports from various regions indicate a rising percentage of adolescents among international migrants. For example 15 percent of all Mexicans seeking to emigrate to in the U.S. in 1997 were adolescents, between 14 and 17 years of age. Studies on the border between Thailand, Myanmar and China report adolescents as young as 13 crossing borders alone. If we extend the definition of youth to also include those who are between the ages of 25 to 29, half of the migrant flow and a third of the stock[3] would be young people.

5   Many receiving countries, in particular those with aging populations, benefit from young international migrants who fill the lowest-paid jobs that no one else wants. They provide manual labor in agriculture and construction; they do domestic work and service jobs in homes, hotels, and restaurants. There is also a growing demand for qualified workers in such areas as health care, communication technologies, and sports.

---

[1]**developing countries** *poorer countries without much industry that are working to improve life for their people*
[2]**developed countries** *rich countries that have many industries and a comfortable lifestyle for most people*
[3]**(migrant) stock** *people living outside their country of birth*

6   The emigration of young people is not always good for the sending countries or the young emigrants. It reduces the number of workers in a highly productive age group, including many who are newly qualified or skilled. When young people emigrate alone, they lose the networks of family and friends that give them support and a sense of identity and direction. However, there can be good results as well. Young emigrants often send money back to their home countries and bring their skills and experience with them if they return.

7   How well international migrants integrate into their host country largely depends on the host countries' policies to help young immigrants learn the language, find employment, housing, education and health care, and protect them from racism, xenophobia, and discrimination. It also depends on a person's ability to adapt. Young people are often more flexible and eager to learn and can help their elders.

rewarding
a. negative
b. positive

8   In spite of the risks of moving abroad, most young people find it a **rewarding** experience, offering employment, increased skills, and knowledge of the world with benefits for both host and home countries.

COMPREHENSION CHECK

First Reading

Answer these questions.

1. Under what circumstances would people who are not yet adults leave their families and emigrate alone?
2. What types of countries do they tend to go to?
3. When young people emigrate, which country or countries benefit: home, host, or both?

STUDY SKILL: TAKING NOTES

Taking notes helps you to identify and remember important facts and details in your academic reading. You can highlight these facts in the text or write them down in a notebook. Doing this will help you to prepare for class discussions and to review for tests. You should take notes when you see the symbol at right.

Second Reading

Read the selection again, and highlight or take notes on a separate piece of paper to answer the questions.

1. What qualities do young people have that help them succeed?
2. In what ways do host countries benefit from having young immigrants?
3. How are their countries of origin affected, both positively and negatively, by emigration?
4. What do emigrants give up, and what might they gain, when they leave their country?

Vocabulary Building

Read the underlined word or expression in its context and match it with the correct meaning. Use a dictionary if necessary.

PART 1

____ 1. Violence . . . or <u>persecution</u> drive many others to escape. (¶1)

____ 2. . . . they take with them the great assets of youth, . . . <u>resourcefulness</u> . . . (¶2)

____ 3. . . . the great assets of youth: . . . <u>perseverance</u>. (¶2)

____ 4. . . . they face <u>obstacles</u> and risks . . . (¶2)

____ 5. . . . risks that test their <u>endurance</u>. (¶2)

____ 6. Young people on the move are <u>determined</u>. (¶3)

a. things that make it difficult to succeed

b. the will to keep trying to do something difficult

c. cruel, unfair treatment for reasons such as nationality, religion, and political beliefs

d. very sure of what they want to do

e. the ability to find ways to deal with problems effectively

f. the ability to suffer difficulties or pain with strength and patience for a long period of time

PART 2

____ 7. Others pay <u>smugglers</u> to get them in. (¶3)

____ 8. They provide <u>manual labor</u> in agriculture and construction. . . . (¶5)

____ 9. There is also a growing demand for <u>qualified</u> workers. . . . (¶5)

____10. How well migrants <u>integrate</u> into their new country depends largely on the host countries' policies. . . . (¶7)

____11. . . . protect them from <u>racism</u> . . . (¶7)

____12. . . . protect them from . . . <u>xenophobia</u> . . . (¶7)

g. become part of a society

h. extreme fear or dislike of people from other countries

i. work with hands that does not need a lot of skill

j. unfair treatment of people because they belong to a different race

k. people who take things or people illegally from one place to another

l. having the right knowledge, experience, and skills for a particular job

Using a Dictionary

Write the number of the meaning in the dictionary entry below that best defines the underlined word as it is used in the sentence. If there is an example sentence, read it carefully to see if it helps you understand the word better. You may want to use the dictionary definition and example sentence if you add some of these words to your word bank. (See page xx of the Introductory Chapter.)

1. . . . they take with them the great <u>assets</u> of youth. . . . (¶2)

   Definition # _____

   > **as·set** /'æsɛt/ *n.* **1** something that a company owns, that can be sold to pay debts **2** someone or something that is useful in helping you succeed or deal with problems: *A sense of humor is a real asset.* | *You're an asset to the company, George.*

2. . . . the great assets of youth, <u>resilience</u>, resourcefulness, and perseverance. (¶2)

   Definition # _____

   > **re·sil·ience** /rɪ'zɪlyəns/ *n.* [U] **1** the ability to quickly become strong, healthy, or happy, after a difficult situation, illness, etc.: *Experts say this is a sign of the economy's resilience.* **2** the ability of a substance such as rubber to return to its usual shape when pressure is removed –**resilient** *adj.*

3. . . . 15 percent of all Mexicans <u>seeking</u> employment . . . (¶4)

   Definition # _____

   > **seek** /sik/ *v.* **sought, sought, seeking 1** [I,T] to try to find or get something: *The UN is seeking a political solution to the crisis.* **2** [T] FORMAL to try to achieve or do something: *The governor will not say whether he will seek re-election next year.* **3 seek advice/help etc.** FORMAL to ask someone for advice, help, etc.

4. . . . they lose the <u>networks</u> of family and friends. . . . (¶6)

   Definition # _____

   > **net·work**[1] /'nɛt lwɚk/ *n.* **1** a group of radio or television stations that broadcasts many of the same programs in different parts of the country: *the four biggest TV networks* **2** a system of lines, tubes, wires, roads, etc. that cross each other and are connected to each other: *the freeway network* **3** a set of computers that are connected to each other so that they can share information **4** a group of people, organization, etc. that are connected or that work together: *Trina had developed a good **network of** business contacts.*

5. . . . depends on the host countries' <u>policies</u> . . . (¶7)

   Definition # _____

   > **pol·i·cy** /'pɑləsi/ *n.* **1** [C,U] a way of doing things that has been officially agreed and chosen by a political party or organization: *the government's foreign policy* | *the company's **policy on** maternity leave* **2** a written agreement with an insurance company: *a homeowner's policy* **3** [C,U] a particular principle that you believe in: *I **make it** my **policy** not to gossip.*

6. . . . protect them from racism,   **Definition #** _____
    xenophobia, and <u>discrimination</u>. (¶7)

> **dis·crim·i·na·tion** /dɪˌskrɪməˈneɪʃən/ *n.* [U] **1** the practice of treating one group of people differently from another in an unfair way: *sex discrimination* | *working to stop* **discrimination against** *the disabled* **2** the ability to judge what is of good quality and what is not

7. Young people are often more   **Definition #** _____
    <u>flexible</u>. . . . (¶7)

> **flex·i·ble** /ˈflɛksəbəl/ *adj.* **1** a person, plan, etc. that is flexible or can change or be changed easily to suit any new situation: *a flexible style of management* **2** something that is flexible can bend or be bent easily: *flexible plastic* **–flexibility** /ˌflɛksəˈbɪləti/ *n.* [U] **–opposite** INFLEXIBLE

8. . . . and <u>eager</u> to learn. (¶7)   **Definition #** _____

> **eager** /ˈigɚ/ *adj.* **1** having a strong desire to do something or a strong interest in something: *I've been* **eager to** *meet you.* | *a young woman* **eager for** *success* **2** **eager to please** willing to do anything that people want **–eagerly** *adv.* **–eagerness** *n.* [U]

Vocabulary Review

Complete the following statements about the reading selection with the correct word or expression from the list below. Use each word or expression only once.

assets	eager	obstacles
better-off	flexible	qualified
discrimination	integrate	rewarding

1. Many emigrants are young people who move without their families to countries that are _____ than their homelands.

2. Although they face many _____, young people tend to have qualities or _____ that help them adapt and _____ into the host society.

3. They may be _____ to fill jobs in areas where there is demand, and many are _____ to learn new skills.

4. In addition, they adapt more successfully than older people because they are _____, resourceful, resilient, and determined to succeed.

5. So in spite of possible _____, they are more likely to find moving abroad a(n) _____ experience.

TEXT ANALYSIS

Paragraph Topics

This selection follows a common type of organization: Introduction, Body, and Conclusion. Match each paragraph or set of paragraphs in the body with its topic.

¶1 Introduction

¶2–3 ___

¶4 ___

¶5 ___

¶6 ___

¶7 ___

¶8 Conclusion

a. benefits to receiving countries

b. integration into the host society

c. details about the characteristics of youth

d. rising number of young migrants

e. losses to country of origin and to individual

RESPONDING TO READING

Discuss these questions.

1. From the decision to leave to the adjustment to life in a new country, what are some difficulties, risks, and rewards of migration?

2. How do host or receiving countries treat immigrants? Do they want them to integrate into the host society or not? Talk about your personal experiences or the experiences of people you know.

CHAPTER 6

ABOUT THE READING

The reading in this chapter is in two parts. Both parts are excerpts from the same source as the reading in Chapter 5, "Moving Young," UNFPA report, *State of World Population*, 2006. The book contains personal stories based on interviews with ten young people who are living the reality of migration.

BEFORE YOU READ

Thinking about the Topic

Discuss these questions.

1. If you have left your country, how old were you when you left? Did you leave with your family or alone? If you are not an immigrant, answer the questions for an immigrant you know.
2. Have families you know of ever been separated because of migration? Was the separation short-term or long-term? How did it affect the family?

Previewing

Look at the maps below and on page 38. Then read the first paragraph of both Part 1: Bibi, and Part 2: Rajini. Which part are you more interested in reading? Why?

Choose one of the parts to read. Before you read, turn to Comprehension Check, First Reading, on page 40. Your purpose for the first reading is to be able to answer the questions for the part you chose.

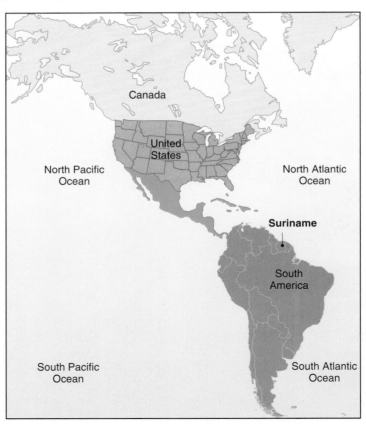

Part 1: Bibi—Surinamese Nurse Trainee

Bibi Sattuar, born in Paramaribo, Suriname in 1983, always knew she wanted to be a nurse. In spite of her mother's objections, she started her nursing studies in 2005, a couple of years after she graduated from high school.

1   In October 2005, Bibi started her courses—a combination of classroom work and hands-on training at Saint Vincentius Hospital. Bibi is quite pleased with the nursing program, although the work can be tough. Five of her thirty-three classmates have already **dropped out of** the program. Bibi does not even consider dropping out, but she complains that her life has become quite difficult. She spends eight hours a day in the hospital and earns only 50 Suriname dollars, about US$18 a month. That is not even enough to cover her transportation costs, **let alone** books and photocopies or the mandatory uniform.[1]

2   Bibi says that the hospital is her whole life. She does not have a boyfriend. Her parents don't want her to, and besides, she says, a boyfriend is "a headache." Now she has to finish her studies and that keeps her busy all the time.

3   INTERVIEWER: And what do you think you'll do when you get your degree?
     BIBI: I will probably leave.
     INTERVIEWER: Leave?
     BIBI: Yes, I'll go abroad.

4   In Suriname, brain drain[2] is a **major** problem in health care: doctors and, above all, nurses leave the country as soon as they can, generally as soon as they finish their studies. Bibi attributes the problem to low pay for medical professionals. The work is hard, but the fact that so many professionals leave makes it even harder. It is a vicious cycle: the more people leave, the more people want to leave because those who stay have to work harder to cover for those who have gone.

5   And there is no **shortage** of opportunities. One of Bibi's aunts is a nurse in Canada. A few month's ago, while Bibi's mother and her aunt were talking on the phone, her mother mentioned that Bibi was attending nursing school. Her aunt replied "Oh, so when she gets her degree she can come here to work with me." Since then Canada has been on the horizon.

6   INTERVIEWER: What do you know about Canada?
     BIBI: Well, nothing. Just that it's very cold there.
     INTERVIEWER: Can you imagine yourself living somewhere else?
     BIBI: Yes, I can imagine myself anywhere. In life you have to have ambition. If not, you get **stuck**. I'm brave and I want to get ahead, so I'm not worried about what life might be like elsewhere.
     INTERVIEWER: But if you go somewhere else, would it just be because they pay you better or are there other reasons as well?
     BIBI: No, there's no other reason. It's just that I work hard and want to be paid what I deserve.

---

[1]**mandatory uniform** *clothing that everyone has to wear in a certain situation such as school or work*
[2]**brain drain** *when the educated people of a country leave for better opportunities abroad*

dropped out of
a. found
b. left

let alone
a. without considering
b. without needing

major
a. big, important
b. small, unimportant

shortage
a. reason
b. lack of

stuck
a. not able to move
b. moving easily

INTERVIEWER:	And if you leave, do you think you will ever come back?
BIBI:	I don't know. I'm going to try to live in some place where life is better. Here it looks like you'll always be stuck in the same place.
INTERVIEWER:	What would a better life be like?
BIBI:	I don't know . . . owning my own home, maybe having a car, being able to **make ends meet**.
INTERVIEWER:	All material things . . .
BIBI:	Yes, the rest comes later.
INTERVIEWER:	But you know there is a need for doctors and nurses here. If you go, you are **contributing** to that problem.
BIBI:	Yes, but I don't care. If I can go, I will.
INTERVIEWER:	You mean, you'd go even though you know that you won't be there while your country needs you?
BIBI:	If they need me, they also have to meet my needs. It should be a give-and-take, shouldn't it?

make ends meet
a. tie things together
b. have enough money for expenses

contributing
a. adding to
b. solving

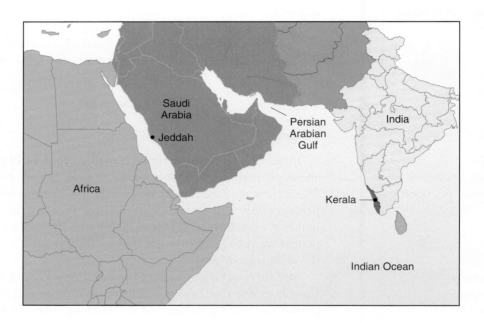

Part 2: Rajini—Indian Gulf Wife

Although she was educated, Rajini had led a very sheltered life: her father made all the decisions for her, and when he died an older brother took over that role. Her marriage to Unnikrishnan was arranged by her family. Their horoscopes[1] matched perfectly, and they were very happy together. However, when Unnikrishnan took a good job in Saudi Arabia, Rajini became a "Gulf wife."

1   More than a million women in the state of Kerala in India live without their husbands who work in the Gulf countries. This means **solitude** but at the same time can be empowering for a young woman. With her husband gone, Rajini was

solitude
a. being alone
b. going to school

[1]**horoscopes** *descriptions of people's futures based on the position of the stars and planets when they were born*

initially
a. finally
b. at first

vacuum
a. cleanliness
b. emptiness

option
a. title
b. choice

evolve
a. change
b. get stuck

wept
a. cried
b. was happy

the one making decisions, handling family finances, running the home, caring for an elderly mother-in-law, and in due time for their baby daughter. "**Initially**," she says, "I was very frightened because I had never done such things before and there was no one to tell me what to do. I just learned from experience, and over time I started to enjoy these responsibilities because I knew I had the full support of my husband in everything I did. So I feel positive, strong and greatly empowered compared to my premarital days when I had absolutely no control over my life."

2   But the real turning point, Rajini says now, was two years ago, when she had to oversee the building of their new house. "The fact that I was able to oversee the construction, handle the workmen, and manage huge amounts of money, have given me the confidence that I can cope with any situation."

3   But this does not make up for the huge emotional **vacuum** in her life. Rajini speaks to her husband almost every day, but she misses him all the time. Rajini and her husband talk about ending this separation; he is not happy being away from her either. But having completed no more than secondary school, there is little chance of Unnikrishnan finding a job in India that would enable him to earn as much as he presently does. And the other **option** of starting his own business, something most migrants dream of doing, will have to wait until they pay back the loan they took to build their house.

4   So Rajini is now hoping that he will be able to find a job in a country that would permit the family to be with him. She says, "I don't think any amount of money can make up for the terrible loneliness that a Gulf wife has to deal with. People who have seen me **evolve**, from being just someone's daughter to a woman who is managing a home and family all by herself, are very impressed . . . but they don't know how lonely I am."

5   Her husband comes home once every two and a half years—for two months. That is why Unnikrishnan could not be there when their daughter was born. "I missed my husband, especially when I was in labor. There was no one to give me moral support and strength the way he would have, and when the baby arrived I **wept** because he was not there to share the moment with me. He saw her for the first time when she was one and a half years old."

6   Unnikrishnan wants to have another child, but Rajini will not consider it unless they live together. And she is concerned with their daughter starting school life without her father. He seems to agree; he wants to be part of her growing up.

7   Rajini dreams of living with her husband, but she is afraid it will not happen anytime soon. Her horoscope told her it was her destiny to be separated from him for some time; astrologers[2] said it could be as long as 17 years.

---

[2]**astrologers** *people who use the movement of stars and planets and their influence on people and events in order to predict the future*

COMPREHENSION CHECK

First Reading

Answer these questions with a partner who read the same part as you. Then work with someone who read the other part and share information about the story and the answers to the questions.

PART 1: **Bibi**

1. How much education does Bibi have?
2. What are her plans?
3. How much does she know about Canada?

PART 2: **Rajini**

1. How has Rajini's life changed since she became a "Gulf wife"?
2. What is the primary benefit of Rajini and Unnikrishnan's situation? What is the primary disadvantage?
3. What do they hope will happen in the future? What do they realistically expect to happen in the future?

Second Reading

Read the selection again, and highlight or take notes to answer the questions.

PART 1: **Bibi**

1. What qualities does Bibi have that should help her succeed? What details can you find to support your answer?

2. How does she feel about her contribution to the brain drain? What does she think countries that are losing their educated youth should do?

PART 2: **Rajini**

1. What are other disadvantages of Rajini and Unnikrishnan's separation?

2. What are the obstacles to Unnikrishnan's returning to India to work? What other alternative is there?

Vocabulary Building

Do the vocabulary matching exercise for the part you read. If you want to learn more vocabulary, do the other part as well. Read the underlined word or expression and match it with the correct meaning. Use a dictionary if necessary.

PART 1: Bibi

___ 1. . . . the work can be <u>tough</u>. (¶1)

___ 2. Bibi <u>attributes</u> the problem to low pay for medical professionals. (¶4)

___ 3. It is a <u>vicious cycle</u>: the more people leave, the more people want to leave. . . . (¶4)

___ 4. Since then Canada has been <u>on the horizon</u>. (¶5)

___ 5. In life you have to have <u>ambition</u>. (¶6)

___ 6. . . . I work hard and want to be paid what I <u>deserve</u>. (¶6)

a. says the cause is, credits

b. likely to happen in the future

c. am worth, should get for what I do

d. desire to succeed or get ahead

e. hard, difficult

f. situation in which one problem causes another problem that then causes the first problem again

PART 2: Rajini

___ 1. This means solitude but at the same time can be <u>empowering</u> for a young woman. (¶1)

___ 2. . . . she had to <u>oversee</u> the building of their new house. (¶2)

___ 3. But this does not <u>make up for</u> the huge emotional vacuum in her life. (¶3)

___ 4. . . . there is little chance of Unnikrishnan finding a job in India that would <u>enable</u> him to earn as much as he presently does. (¶3)

___ 5. People . . . <u>are</u> very <u>impressed</u>. . . . (¶4)

___ 6. . . . it was her <u>destiny</u> to be separated from him for some time. . . . (¶7)

a. feel admiration and respect

b. fate, what will happen in the future

c. supervise, watch workers to make sure that work is done correctly

d. giving someone power, confidence, or the right to do something

e. make it possible for, make (him) able

f. compensate for, make a bad situation seem better

Vocabulary Review

Complete the following statements about the reading selection with the correct word or expression from the list below. Use each word or expression only once.

PART 1: **Bibi**

ambitious

contributing

make ends meet

on the horizon

tougher

vicious cycle

PART 2: **Rajini**

destiny

empowering

evolve

impressed

make up for

oversee

PART 1

1. Bibi is in a nursing program in Suriname, and a career in Canada is

   _____.

2. She knows she will be _____ to the brain drain, which is affecting health care in many developing countries. The brain drain creates a(n) _____ that leaves Suriname without enough nurses and doctors. For those who remain, their jobs become even

   _____.

3. Bibi is a(n) _____ woman and wants to get ahead. On the salary she could get in Suriname, it is not possible to _____, and she would like to have a better life.

PART 2

1. Rajini has not migrated from India, but her husband works in Saudi Arabia. In spite of the loneliness, she has found that the situation has been _____ for her, especially when she had to _____ the building of their house by herself.

2. Her situation has helped her _____ into a more confident, capable person in control of her own life. People are _____ with the woman she has become.

3. But she feels that nothing can _____ her solitude and loneliness.

4. Both Rajini and Unnikrishnan would like to end their separation, but living far from each other may be their _____ for some time to come.

TEXT ANALYSIS   *Cause and Effect*

A *cause* is the source or origin of a condition or situation; an *effect* is the result of the condition or situation. *A* can be the direct cause of *B*, or it can be one factor contributing to *B*, the effect. An effect may in turn become a cause of something else. For example, low pay causes many people to leave their country; this brain drain then becomes the cause of even worse conditions in the developing country (a vicious cycle). There are several words and phrases that show a cause and effect relationship, including *because, so, as a result,* and *therefore.*

Work with a partner who read the part you did not read. Complete the following sentences with the effect that is a consequence of the cause in the first clause.

PART **1**

1. Nurses earn very little money in Suriname, so Bibi

   _____.

2. Because so many nurses and doctors leave Suriname to work abroad,

   _____.

3. Bibi's aunt is a nurse in Canada; therefore, Bibi

   _____.

PART **2**

4. Rajini's husband has only a high school degree; as a result, he

   _____.

5. Because Rajini's husband lives far away,

   _____.

6. Rajini's husband wasn't in India when they built a house; as a result,

   _____.

RESPONDING TO READING

Discuss these questions as a whole class. Ask appropriate questions to clarify anything you do not understand about the part you didn't read.

1. What do you think of Bibi's attitude about leaving her country? Should she care about the need for nurses in Suriname? Do you think she will be able to adapt to Canada? Is it a good idea for her to migrate alone?

2. Would you be willing to accept separation from a spouse in a situation similar to Rajini and Unnikrishnan's? Why or why not? Do you think they should have another child? Why or why not?

"Bosnia's Loss Is an American City's Gain" appeared in the Grass-Roots Business section of the *New York Times* on April 25, 1999. The author, Joel Kotkin, is a senior fellow at the Pepperdine Institute for Public Policy.

**BEFORE
YOU READ**

Thinking about the Topic

Discuss these questions.

1. When ethnic groups migrate, they often settle near people from the same group. Why do you think they do this?
2. What advantages or disadvantages might ethnic communities have for both the immigrants and the communities they settle in?

Previewing

Read the first paragraph and the first sentence of the second paragraph, and answer the questions.

1. During most of the 1990s, the Bevo neighborhood in St. Louis was

   a. busy, doing well economically.

   b. in bad condition, economically depressed.

2. The neighborhood changed when

   a. immigrants left the neighborhood.

   b. immigrants moved into the area.

Before you read, turn to Comprehension Check, First Reading, on page 46. Your purpose for the first reading is to be able to answer those questions.

READ

Bosnia's Loss Is an American City's Gain *By Joel Kotkin*

shrinking
a. getting bigger
b. getting smaller

1   For most of the 1990's, the Southern Commercial Bank branch on Gravois Avenue, where Steve Hrdlicka is a loan officer, was a forlorn place, stuck in an aging neighborhood in a **shrinking** city. New accounts were few, and the empty stores along Gravois and other once-bustling streets in the Bevo neighborhood of south St. Louis suggested little hope for the future.

2   All that changed when a stream of new immigrants, largely Bosnians leaving behind the ethnic conflicts in the former Yugoslavia, began settling in this unlikely

part of the Midwest.[1] "Eight years ago when we opened this branch, we sat on our hands most of the time—we used to sleep quite a lot," recalled Mr. Hrdlicka (pronounced HERD-lick-a), now 39, who grew up in the mostly white, working-class south St. Louis, the great-grandson of Czech immigrants. "Then this place became a rally place[2] for Bosnians. They would come in and ask for a loan for furniture. Then a car. Then it was a house, for themselves, their cousins."

3   Largely thanks to the Bosnian newcomers, who have developed a reputation for hard work and thrift, Mr. Hrdlicka's branch has doubled its deposits in the last two years.

4   For greater St. Louis, an unexpected opportunity for revival has come with the arrival of an estimated 15,000 Bosnian immigrants in the 1990's—a concentration second in size only to Chicago's—along with smaller groups of newcomers from Mexico, Vietnam, Ethiopia and Somalia.

5   This kind of story of hard-working immigrants revitalizing a **sagging** urban neighborhood is a familiar one in immigrant havens[3] like New York or Houston. But it is big news in St. Louis, which has not received new immigrants for half a century.

6   In the late 1800's, new arrivals from Germany, Ireland, Italy, and Eastern Europe were building St. Louis into an industrial and commercial metropolis similar to Chicago. But after World War II, the city lost its **appeal** to ambitious newcomers.

7   Since 1950, the population of the city has **shriveled** from 857,000 to roughly 350,000, proportionally the sharpest decline of any major American city. This decline is due in large part to the fact that the movement of people to suburban areas[4] around St. Louis and to other parts of the country has not been balanced by immigration from abroad, as it has in New York or Los Angeles.

8   On the south side of St. Louis, historically an immigrant district, old brick owner-occupied homes were gradually becoming rentals, and thriving commercial districts were slowly being abandoned. Prices for homes, stores, factory buildings, and warehouses **plummeted**.

9   But those **depressed** conditions have made possible the current upsurge in Bosnian immigration, according to Ann Crosslin, president of the International Institute of St. Louis, a nonprofit group that aids refugees[5] and promotes

---

sagging
a. becoming less valuable
b. improving, getting strong

appeal
a. attraction
b. reason

shriveled
a. gotten larger
b. gotten smaller

plummeted
a. went up a lot
b. went down a lot

depressed
a. economically good
b. economically bad

---

[1]**Midwest** *the area in the middle of the United States, including Missouri, where St. Louis is located (see map at right)*
[2]**rally place** *a place that brings people together, meaning that many Bosnians were coming together in St. Louis*
[3]**havens** *originally meant "harbors," now places people go to be safe or happy*
[4]**suburban areas** *residential areas surrounding major cities, usually small towns, which together with the major city form a metropolitan area*
[5]**refugees** *people who have been forced to leave their country, especially during a war*

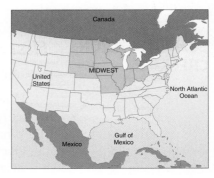

international cultural programs in the city. She said the small first wave of refugees, in the early 1990's, found housing costs so low—a two-bedroom apartment in Bevo rents for roughly $400 a month, and $50,000 buys a decent house—that the area soon attracted fellow Bosnians who had first landed in other places.

10   "St. Louis is seen as a cheap place to live," noted Jasna Mruckovski, a refugee from Banja Luka, the Bosnian Serb capital, who arrived in St. Louis in 1994. "People come from California, Chicago and Florida, where it's more expensive. Bosnians don't care if they start by buying the smallest, ugliest house. At least they feel they have something."

11   Ms. Mruckovski (pronounced muh-ruh-KOV-ski), 25, should know. By day a translator in Southern Commercial's Bevo branch, she moonlights as a real estate agent[6] and has helped sell 33 homes in the area over the last year, all but one to Bosnian buyers. In many cases, she said, whole families including children pooled wages to buy those homes.

12   The willingness of Bosnian immigrants to work hard at two or even three jobs is becoming well-known among local employers. With unemployment in the region only slightly over 3 percent, there are many job opportunities. At Willert Home Products, a third of the 320 employees are immigrants.

13   "You want to find employees with a good work ethic, and the refugees are about the best," said W. D. Willert, president of the company. "We now have 12 nationalities here, and when we need more workers, we know the Bosnians will call their cousins."

on welfare
a. receiving money from the government
b. using the hospitals

14   Almost no immigrants in the St. Louis area are **on welfare.** Of the estimated 17,000 families receiving benefits through Aid to Families with Dependent Children, the largest welfare program, just 40 are foreign-born, according to Ms. Crosslin.

15   Like many other immigrant groups before them, the Bosnians will probably have an increasing impact on their new home as business owners. Bosnian immigrants have already started a trucking company and dozens of Bosnian restaurants, shops, and grocery stores.

---

[6]**moonlights as a real estate agent** *has a second job selling houses and land*

COMPREHENSION CHECK

First Reading

Answer these questions with a partner.

1. How did business at the Gravois Avenue branch of the bank change from the early to late 1990s?
2. What turned the situation around?
3. Overall, what kind of impact, or effect, have the Bosnians had on their new neighborhood and city?

Second Reading

A. Read the selection again. Then complete the chart with details from the reading that answer the prompts on the left.

	Late 1800s–1950	1950–Early 1990s	Later 1990s
1. What immigrant groups, if any, came to St. Louis?		Immigrant flow stopped (¶6)	
2. Describe the economy of the city.	Industrial, commercial metropolis (¶6)		
3. How much did the population of St. Louis grow or shrink?		(¶7)	

B. Highlight or take notes to answer the questions.

1. Why was St. Louis attractive to the Bosnians?
2. What characteristics account for the success of the Bosnians and their contribution to the Bevo neighborhood?

Vocabulary Building

Read the underlined word or expression in its context and match it with the correct meaning. Use a dictionary if necessary.

PART 1

____ 1. . . . the Southern Commercial Bank branch on Gravois Avenue . . . was a <u>forlorn</u> place, stuck in an aging neighborhood. . . . (¶1)

____ 2. . . . Bosnians leaving behind the <u>ethnic conflicts</u> in the former Yugoslavia . . . (¶2)

____ 3. . . . Bosnian newcomers . . . have developed a <u>reputation</u> for hard work. . . . (¶3)

____ 4. . . . hard work and <u>thrift</u> . . . (¶3)

____ 5. . . . Hrdlicka's branch has doubled its <u>deposits</u> in the last two years. (¶3)

____ 6. . . . an estimated 15,000 Bosnian immigrants in the 1990's—a <u>concentration</u> second in size only to Chicago's . . . (¶4)

a. careful use of money

b. opinion people have of someone or something, what they are known for

c. money put in the bank

d. sad, lonely

e. large number in the same place

f. disagreements or wars between races, nations, tribes, or religious groups

PART 2

____ 7. . . . the population of the city has shriveled from 857,000 to roughly 350,000, <u>proportionally</u> the sharpest decline of any major American city. (¶7)

____ 8. . . . <u>thriving</u> commercial districts were slowly being abandoned. (¶8)

____ 9. . . . a nonprofit group that aids refugees and <u>promotes</u> international cultural programs in the city. . . . (¶9)

____10. . . . $50,000 buys a <u>decent</u> house. . . . (¶9)

____11. . . . whole families including children <u>pooled wages</u> to buy those homes. (¶11)

____12. . . . find employees with a good <u>work ethic</u> . . . (¶13)

g. successful, doing well

h. acceptable, good enough

i. in relation to its size

j. combined their money to be able to use it

k. beliefs about work

l. arranges public events for

Word Parts

One way to handle unfamiliar vocabulary is to look for parts of words whose meaning you know. A word like *hard-working*, as in "hard-working immigrants" (¶5), is easy. <u>*Hard-working* means "people who work hard."</u>

Sometimes you get help from only one part, such as *once* in *once-bustling*. (¶1) You probably know that *once* means "at some time in the past." You probably would have to use your dictionary for *bustling,* which means "busy."

Sometimes knowledge of Latin and Greek roots will help. For example, *metropolis* (¶6) comes from the Greek words *mete* "mother" + *polis* "city." <u>*Metropolis* means "large city."</u>

Analyze the underlined words in the sentences and write their meanings on the lines. The word parts below will help you figure out what some of the words mean. Make sure your definition makes sense in the sentence.

> *re*—do again
>
> *un*—not (reverses the meaning of the base word)
>
> *vivere* (Latin)—live
>
> *vita* (Latin)—life

1. Largely thanks to the Bosnian <u>newcomers</u> . . . (¶3) _____

2. . . . an <u>unexpected</u> opportunity . . . (¶4) _____

3. . . . an unexpected opportunity for <u>revival</u> has come with the arrival of an estimated 15,000 Bosnian immigrants. . . . (¶4) _____

4. . . . hard-working immigrants <u>revitalizing</u> a sagging urban neighborhood . . . (¶5) _____

5. With <u>unemployment</u> in the region only slightly over 3 percent . . . (¶12) _____

Vocabulary Review

Complete the following statements about the reading selection with the correct word or expression from the list below. Use each word or expression only once.

decent	revitalize	thriving	welfare
newcomers	revival	unemployment	work ethic
pooling			

1. Bosnian refugees fleeing ethnic conflict in the former Yugoslavia have helped _____ the city of St. Louis, Missouri.

2. One hundred years ago, St. Louis was a _____ metropolis with a vibrant immigrant population. But as the immigrants integrated into American society and moved to the suburbs, the city fell into an economic depression.

3. The Bosnians who arrived in the 1990s have a strong

_____. They are hard-working employees, and some have

started their own businesses.

4. St. Louis was a land of opportunity for these _____. Real

estate prices were low, and they could afford to buy _____

homes by _____ the wages of the whole family.

5. Now _____ in the city is low, and very few foreign-born

residents are on _____. At least the Bevo neighborhood is

enjoying a _____.

Journalistic Writing

Journalists are trained to communicate information objectively and quickly. As a result, their writing often has the following characteristics:

a. it gives facts, not opinion or interpretation
b. it has short sentences—fifteen words or fewer
c. it has short paragraphs—three sentences or fewer

One reason for the short paragraphs is that newspaper text is usually set in narrow columns; long paragraphs in narrow columns would look strange and be difficult to read.

Review the text in order to answer the following questions.

1. Does the writer give facts only, without opinion or interpretation?
2. Are most of the sentences short (fifteen words or fewer)?
3. Are most of the paragraphs short (three sentences or fewer)?
4. Is this article typical of journalistic writing?

RESPONDING TO READING **Discuss these questions.**

1. What do you think the nonimmigrant residents of St. Louis think of their new immigrant population?

2. Compare the description of the Bosnian immigrants in this article to immigrant groups you know. In what ways are they similar? In what ways are they different?

3. What contributions have other immigrant groups made to their communities?

ABOUT THE READING

"(Un)American" is an excerpt from one of the personal essays in *Waking Up American: Coming of Age Biculturally.* Tumang, the author, is the daughter of immigrants from the Philippines.

BEFORE YOU READ

Thinking about the Topic

Discuss these questions.

1. What happens to the children of immigrants in terms of integration into the host society?
2. Think about the poem on the introductory page of this unit. How are the children of immigrants like a door between two worlds?

Previewing

Read the first paragraph of this selection, and answer these questions.

1. Does the author believe it is easy to be bicultural?
2. As the child of immigrants, who does she want to be accepted by?

Before you read, turn to Comprehension Check, First Reading, on page 53. Your purpose for the first reading is to be able to answer those questions.

READ

(Un)American *By Patricia Justine Tumang*

1   Trying to combine my two cultures was like mixing oil with water—no matter how much I tried to mix my Filipino and American identities, they always separated. . . . When I was a child I wanted more than anything to be accepted both by my family and by my American peers at school.

2   Bringing packed lunches to elementary school signaled my difference. Although many of my classmates were kids of color—black, Latino, and Asian—white students viewed anything not considered American as strange. Instead of baloney[1] and cheese sandwiches, a typical American lunch, I ate rice and my mother's chicken adobo.[2] "You eat rice with every meal?" a white classmate once asked me. "Yes," I responded. *Didn't everybody?* "That's weird," she said. It wasn't weird to me. "What is that stuff?" she asked. "It's adobo." I said. A confused look on her face told me that she didn't understand. "It's chicken," I added, "and it's really good." Feeling satisfied with my answer, my classmate continued eating her lunch. I hadn't realized until that point that no one knew what chicken adobo was. Suddenly I felt like an outsider.

---

[1]**baloney** *a type of cooked meat usually put in sandwiches*
[2]**chicken adobo** *Filipino-style chicken made in a sauce using vinegar, soy sauce, garlic, pepper, and bay leaf*

was left in the dark
a. understood
b. didn't understand

belted out
a. sang loudly
b. talked about

lyrics
a. musical notes
b. words

extended dialogues
a. long conversations
b. long letters

ashamed
a. embarrassed
b. proud

distinct
a. the same
b. different

3   And in some ways, I felt like an outsider at home, too. Growing up, I felt different from my Filipino parents, who immigrated to the United States a year before I was born. I didn't grow up speaking Tagalog like my parents did. When I was a little girl, my parents exchanged audiotapes with our relatives in the Philippines instead of calling or writing letters. When our relatives sent us audiotapes their voices filled our stereo with sounds that were unfamiliar to me. . . .

4   English was inserted only sporadically, so I **was left in the dark**. "What are they saying?" I'd ask my mom, persistently tugging on her sleeve. "Shhhh," she'd say and hug me affectionately. "Please quiet, I want to hear what they're saying. It's just *tsismis*[3] anyway." A smile spread over her face as she listened to the latest gossip. Sometimes tears streamed down her cheeks when she heard her mother speak. What happy news was shared? Did something bad happen to our family? I didn't know how to articulate such questions yet.

5   The joys and longings my parents experienced were transferred to me as I sang unabashedly in Tagalog. In fact, the only Tagalog I knew was from Filipino songs on tapes sent by my mother's brothers, who were musicians. The Filipino ballads[4] that we listened to in the house became part of the background as my mother cooked Filipino food and I did homework at night. My mother told me that the songs were about longing and heartache. I'd sing the tunes as easily as I would "Old McDonald Had a Farm,"[5] and my parents would tape me and send these audiotapes to our relatives in the Philippines. I **belted out** the chorus to the Filipino songs with gusto[6] and feeling, wondering if my voice could carry through to the other side, seven thousand miles across ocean and land, to the place that my parents called home.

6   I can only imagine how my relatives would have reacted to me singing. Tita Carina, my mother's sister-in-law, would have said, "Look at how cute she is, she actually knows all of the words." Tito Eddieboy, one of my mother's brothers, would have laughed and felt proud since the songs I sang were his favorites by the Filipino singer Basil Valdez. I wonder if while listening to the tapes, they noticed my American accent. I wonder if it occurred to them that I had no idea what the **lyrics** meant.

7   Our audiotapes became **extended dialogues** that replaced expensive phone calls. My uncles would make *tugon,* which in Ilonggo means to make a request, and it was usually for name-brand shirts, such as Lacoste or Polo; Hormel corned-beef hash; Spam; Whitman's chocolates; and American music.

8   Tita Carina's voice was singsong and childlike as she tried imitating me. "Oh my god, Patricia. I am so American now. Dude."[7] My parents laughed even though I didn't think it was funny. A large part of me felt **ashamed** that I couldn't relate to my relatives in the same way that my parents did. I wanted to feel a connection to my family and Filipino culture.

9   I was Filipino in a different way from my family. I didn't know how to speak Tagalog; I didn't understand any of their stories and jokes. The America I grew up in was made of Barbie dolls, McDonald's, and Saturday-morning cartoons like *Thundercats, Smurfs* and *Lady Lovely Locks.* But I didn't feel that this America resonated wholly with who I was. Certainly none of these cartoon characters represented my bilingual family. The two identities that I was struggling to unite—American and Filipino—were separate and **distinct**.

---

[3]**tsismis** *Tagalog word for unimportant talk, gossip*
[4]**ballads** *songs, usually about love*
[5]**"Old McDonald Had a Farm"** *common American children's song that teaches the names of animals and the sounds they make*

[6]**with gusto** *eager enjoyment, enthusiastically*
[7]**dude** *slang, used to address a male or a female (similar to* guy*)*

First Reading

Answer these questions.

1. What do Patricia's American classmates do to make her feel like an outsider?
2. What contact does she have with her Filipino relatives?

Second Reading

Read the selection again and answer the questions.

1. In what ways is Patricia neither completely American nor completely Filipino?

2. The topic of this selection is

   a. becoming American.

   b. losing your mother tongue.

   c. trying to unite two identities.

3. What is the main idea of the selection?

   a. It was difficult for Patricia to combine her two identities: Filipino and American.

   b. Patricia was equally comfortable in Filipino and American culture.

   c. The children of immigrants easily become bicultural.

Vocabulary Building

Read the underlined word or expression in its context and match it with the correct meaning. Use a dictionary if necessary.

____ 1. Bringing packed lunches to elementary school <u>signaled</u> my difference. (¶2)

____ 2. Suddenly I felt like an <u>outsider</u>. (¶2)

____ 3. English was <u>inserted</u> only sporadically. . . . (¶4)

____ 4. English was inserted only <u>sporadically</u>. . . . (¶4)

____ 5. . . . <u>persistently tugging</u> on her sleeve. (¶4)

____ 6. . . . she listened to the latest <u>gossip</u>. (¶4)

____ 7. I didn't know how to <u>articulate</u> such questions yet. (¶4)

____ 8. The joys and <u>longings</u> my parents experienced . . . (¶5)

____ 9. The joys and longings . . . were <u>transferred</u> to me as I sang. . . . (¶5)

____10. But I didn't feel that this America <u>resonated</u> wholly <u>with</u> who I was. (¶9)

a. information about people that is not necessarily true

b. only in a few places

c. express

d. someone who is not part of a group

e. had special meaning because it related to one's experience

f. continuously pulling

g. moved, shifted

h. was a sign of, proved, showed

i. desires, strong feelings of wanting

j. put in

Vocabulary Review

Complete the following statements about the reading selection with the correct word or expression from the list below. Use each word or expression only once.

ashamed
distinct

lyrics
outsider

resonate
signaled

1. As a young child, Patricia truly lived between two worlds and felt like a(n) _____ in both. Her chicken adobo lunches _____ her difference from her American classmates.

2. She felt _____ because she didn't feel connected to her Filipino relatives.

3. She knew the _____ to many Filipino songs and sang them with gusto even though she didn't understand Tagalog.

4. She grew up with American culture (Barbie dolls and American cartoons on TV), but those aspects of American culture didn't _____ with who she was either.

5. She was bicultural, but both cultures remained _____.

TEXT ANALYSIS *Unity*

> A paragraph, a short piece of writing—or a section of a longer piece of writing—should be unified; that is, it should deal with one topic. All the ideas in it should have something to do with that topic.

Answer these questions to reveal the unity of "(Un)American," which is a section of a longer piece of writing.

1. How does each paragraph or group of paragraphs contribute to the unity of this piece of writing?

   ¶1 *Introduces the main idea that Tumang's two cultures don't mix—like* *oil and water*

   ¶2 _____

   ¶3–8 _____

2. What does paragraph 9 do for the whole piece of writing? _____

   _____

   _____

RESPONDING TO READING

Discuss these questions.

1. What are some advantages and disadvantages of being bicultural?

2. How do you feel about the children of immigrants maintaining their parents' language, which Tumang did not do?

3. Which metaphor do you prefer to describe being between two worlds: Rao's door metaphor on the introductory page of this unit or Tumang's oil and water metaphor in this chapter? Explain.

UNIT WRAP-UP

Extending Your Vocabulary

Word Families

Study the chart below to learn other forms of some of the words in this unit. If there is a box with a dash, either there is no word to fill it in or the word is missing because it is not one you need to know now.

	NOUNS	VERBS	ADJECTIVES	ADVERBS
1.	ambition	—	ambitious	—
2.	discrimination	discriminate	discriminatory	—
3.	employment unemployment employer employee	employ	employed unemployed	—
4.	flexibility inflexibility	—	flexible inflexible	flexibly
5.	migrant, migration emigrant, emigration immigrant, immigration	migrate emigrate immigrate	migratory migrant	—
6.	qualification	qualify	qualified	—
7.	resilience	—	resilient	resiliently
8.	revival	revive	—	—

For each item below, look at the row in the chart above with the same number. Choose the word that correctly completes the sentence. Be sure to use the correct form.

1. Getting ahead is important for _____ people.

2. Employers should not have _____ policies that work against immigrant and minority groups.

(continued)

Chapter 8   **55**

3. In the late 1990s, the _____ rate in St. Louis was low; there were a lot of job opportunities. Companies _____ many immigrants because they were hard workers.

4. If you are adapting to a new culture, _____ is an important asset. You need to be _____ in new situations.

5. _____ policy is a controversial issue in many countries. Some receiving countries welcome _____, while others want to limit their numbers.

6. Do you have the _____ for the job you are applying for? No one will employ you if you are not _____.

7. When you face obstacles in life, it is helpful to be _____ and not to let problems keep you down.

8. You look very tired. Why don't you take a quick swim? That will _____ you.

Collocations

In any language, certain words combine frequently with other words. These combinations are called *collocations*. One way to improve your vocabulary is to learn new collocations for words. Study the chart below.

cross (v.)	**cross** a boundary, a border, a bridge*, a river, a street, an ocean
handle (v.)	**handle** finances, people, a workload, myself (yourself, herself)
pool (v.)	**pool** ideas, money, resources, wages
run (v.)	**run** a business, a machine, a school, your life, the world
seek (v.)	**seek** advice, approval, employment, help, solutions, the truth, a better life
eager to (adj.)	**eager to** buy, finish, know, learn, leave, meet, share, start
thriving (adj.)	**thriving** business, metropolis, neighborhood
sense of (n.)	**sense of** belonging, dignity, direction, humor, identity, purpose, responsibility, self

There is a saying: "Cross that bridge when you come to it." It means that you should not think or worry about something until it actually happens.

Complete the sentences below with the appropriate collocations. Look at the chart on page 56 for help. There may be more than one correct collocation for some sentences.

1. Have you ever crossed the _____ between Mexico and the United States?

2. Let's cross that _____ when we get to it.

3. As a Gulf wife Rajini learned to handle family _____.

4. She also learned to handle _____ in a more confident way.

5. If we pool our _____, we can rebuild several homes that were damaged in the earthquake.

6. Joseph works in a factory where he runs _____ that cuts out auto parts. His son wants to be independent and run his own _____.

7. When you have a problem, there are various ways to seek _____.

8. Many migrants leave their homeland in order to seek _____ in a country that offers more opportunities.

9. Bibi is eager to _____ Suriname. She is eager to _____ a new life.

10. It is encouraging to see a depressed area become a thriving _____.

11. I always get lost. I don't have a very good sense of _____.

WRITING

Choose one of the suggestions below for writing. Talk about what you plan to write with a classmate who chose the same topic. Then follow the instructions for writing.

1. Write about a professional person you know who has left his or her country to work abroad. Use these questions as a guide:

   a. What education does the person have?
   b. Why did they leave?
   c. Where did they go?
   d. How do they feel about the action they took?
   e. What do they do for their relatives at home?

2. Write your reaction to the poem on the introductory page. Does the door metaphor make sense? Do you think Rao's description is accurate? Support your answer with examples from personal experience.

Try to use some of the following vocabulary in writing about the topic you choose: *ambition, better-off, brain drain, contribute, decent, depressed, destination, determined, discriminate, eager, employment, empowering, enable, flexible, make ends meet, obstacles, on welfare, outsider, qualified, resourceful, rewarding, stuck, tough, work ethic.*

High Tech—Pros and Cons

Discuss

1. What are some of the advantages of modern technology? How does it change lives?
2. What are some of the disadvantages, problems, or dangers of modern technology?

> *I like to play indoors better 'cause that's where all the electrical outlets are.*
>
> A fourth grader cited in *Last Child in the Woods,* by Richard Louv

"Multitasking Madness" is from the September 2007 issue of *Choices,* an American magazine for high school students. Young people today are called Generation M. Many people mistakenly think it means Generation Multitasking because young people seem to be skillful at doing several things at the same time. However, it actually means Generation Millennium and refers to young people growing up in the twenty-first century.

BEFORE YOU READ

Thinking about the Topic

Examine the graphs and facts below. Then discuss the questions that follow.

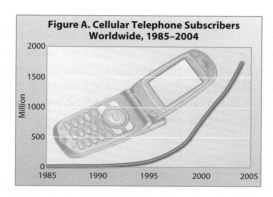

Figure A. Cellular Telephone Subscribers Worldwide, 1985–2004

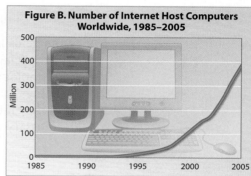

Figure B. Number of Internet Host Computers Worldwide, 1985–2005

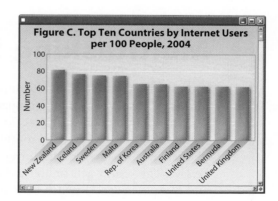

Figure C. Top Ten Countries by Internet Users per 100 People, 2004

Facts:

- While 15 countries have more than 90 cell phone subscribers per 100 residents, more than 40 countries still have fewer than 10 per 100 inhabitants.
- Some 19 countries count more than 50 Internet users per 100 people, while in another 100 countries, less than 10 percent of the population logs on.
- Germany has more than twice as many Internet users as the whole African continent.

Sources: The source for the facts in this box and Figures A and C is the International Telecommunications Union (ITU); the source for Figure B is Internet Systems Consortium. All were reproduced in *Vital Signs* 2006–2007, a publication of the Worldwatch Institute.

1. According to these graphs, when did mobile phone and Internet use really take off?
2. Based on Figure C and the facts in the bulleted list, what can you say about the distribution of Internet access around the world?
3. How does access to high technology, such as the Internet and cell phones, change people's lives? Has it affected your life? If so, how?
4. When you do your homework or study for a test, what other things, if any, do you do *simultaneously*—that is, at the same time?

Previewing

Read the title and the first paragraph, and answer the questions.

1. What is multitasking? What two parts of the word tell you what it means?
2. Do you predict that the author is in favor of multitasking or against it? What words does she use that help you decide?

USING A GLOSSARY

Many fields have technical vocabulary that may be new to you. A glossary is a list of special words with their meanings. There is a glossary of words related to technology and computers on pages 82–83. Check the glossary for the meanings of the following words from the first paragraph if you don't know what they mean: *online, download,* and *text message.* Throughout this unit, use the glossary as needed.

Before you read, turn to Comprehension Check, First Reading, on page 62. Your purpose for the first reading is to be able to answer those questions.

READ

Multitasking Madness *By Leah Paulos*

Are you always online, downloading music, chatting with friends, and sending text messages? If so, you're being trapped by your own technology.

1   When it's time for Andy MacDonald, 17, of Kewaskum, Wisconsin, to do his homework, he follows a daily routine. "I sit down in my living room, put my cell phone down next to me, and turn on the TV shows I recorded the night before," he says. Then Andy gets online and opens up his e-mail account, instant messenger, and MySpace page. "I switch back and forth between work and the other stuff the whole time," he says. "Otherwise, I find it hard to concentrate. Plus, I hate to be out of touch with my friends."

2   It's likely that you and your friends understand the kind of multitasking that Andy engages in quite well. That's because most teens spend **tons of** time connected to the Internet and using all sorts of digital media and technology. According to the Pew Internet and American Life Project, about 87 percent of teens used the Internet in 2005 and half of them went online daily.

tons of
a. a lot of
b. very little

BY THE NUMBERS

3   A 2006 study by Teenage Research Unlimited reported that 19 million American teens instant message and 60 percent have their own cell phones. The Kaiser Family Foundation reported that 13 percent of young people use a handheld device so they can connect to the Internet at any time. Teens also spend an average of six-and-a-half hours a day online!

overusing
a. finished using
b. using too much

solely
a. only
b. quickly

sequentially
a. at the same time
b. one after the other

efficiently
a. slowly
b. well

anxious
a. busy
b. nervous

4   You might think that computers, the Internet, IMing, MP3s, and cell phones are all cool inventions that help make life fun. The problem, though, isn't the technology; it's how people use the technology. Basically, they're **overusing** cell phones, computers, MP3 players, etc.

5   According to the Kaiser study, there's something about computers with high-speed connections that causes obsessive multitasking. You log on and check your e-mail; in the moment you have while downloading pictures, you text a friend to say you'll upload the photo to Facebook ASAP.[1] While doing that, you check the next day's weather online, then click on a video clip on YouTube—all the while listening to the songs you downloaded onto your iPod last week and trying to memorize Spanish verb conjugations. The Kaiser study reports that 26 percent of the time teens spend on digital media is spent multitasking on multiple forms of it. And close to two-thirds of students between the ages of 8 and 18 don't concentrate **solely** on their homework some or most of the time.

BRAIN DRAIN

6   Many people, both teens and adults, think that multitasking is the best way to accomplish a lot in a small amount of time. But scientific evidence says this isn't true. "When people try to perform two or more related tasks, either at the same time or quickly switching back and forth between them, they do a worse job on both of them," says David E. Meyer, director of the Brain, Cognition, and Action Laboratory at the University of Michigan. "They make more errors and it takes them much longer than if they worked on the tasks **sequentially**."

7   Meyer says it can take up to 400 percent longer to do a homework assignment if you're trying to do something else, such as conducting an IM conversation at the same time. Why is this? "The human brain is simply not wired to process more than one complex task at a time," Meyer says. "In the same way that you can't be talking about two different things simultaneously, your brain cannot process two different complex things at the same time."

8   What your brain does instead is prioritize tasks. So if you're listening to music and reading a book, your brain will concentrate on the music, and when that's finished, it will focus on taking in the information from the book. "But it takes a lot of mental energy for your brain to keep reorienting itself back to each task," Meyer says. The result is that neither task is done **efficiently**.

MAKE IT SIMPLE

9   So is it impossible to do two things well at once? No, but the competing tasks can't be too complicated. For instance, you can walk and talk on a cell phone simultaneously. (Just don't do it crossing a street when you need to do a third task—pay attention to traffic.) A way to figure out if you're taking on too much is if you need to do at least one of the tasks repeatedly to get it right.

10   Here's something else to consider: Multitasking not only makes it harder to do things well, it can also stress you out. "The brain can't process two things at once," says Ned Hallowell, a psychiatrist and the author of *CrazyBusy*. "When you continue to try, and fail, it can make you **anxious** and angry."

11   Finally, spending all that time with your gadgets takes away from face-to-face time with actual humans. Yes, it's possible to have safe friendships with peers through the Internet, but it's bad to conduct your entire social life online. "Relationships require some real-life, face-to-face interactions," Hallowell says. "It's harder to create the depth of feeling when you are only sharing fast-paced electronic moments."

(continued)

---

[1]**ASAP** *as soon as possible*

12   Andy MacDonald admits that his habit of multitasking keeps him from hanging out with his friends in person, but "it's hard, because my friends are all online just as much as I am," he says.

GAINING CONTROL

13   Are Andy and the thousands of teens like him doomed to a life chained[2] to technology? No. The key, says Hallowell, is to "use technology to benefit your life, without letting it control it." Here's what you can do:

Set aside two blocks of time. Use one for your Internet and cell phone needs and the other one for studying and homework. Keep them separate. For instance, if you're doing homework on the computer, close all unnecessary Internet browsers.

Control your online social life. If you have 120 MySpace pals, be realistic with how you communicate with them. Don't try to keep in touch with all of them like they're BFFs[3].

Don't eat in front of the computer. Finishing your dinner in the time it takes to upload digital pictures is a sign that you're a tech addict.

Unplug once in a while. Go for a walk, hang out with friends and family in person, read a book, do some artwork, or just daydream.

14   Believe it or not, teens can break free from their gadgets. "Now I turn off my computer and cell phone every day from 4 to 6 P.M. when I study," says Brittany Pringle, 16, of Mena, Arkansas. "It's amazing how much more time I have to see friends and go to basketball games."

---

[2]**chained** *addicted to*   [3]**BFFs** *best friends forever*

COMPREHENSION CHECK

First Reading

Answer these questions.

1. When people multitask, are they doing several things at the same time, or are they switching back and forth?
2. What are the benefits for Brittany Pringle of limiting her cell phone and computer use?

Second Reading

Read the selection again and highlight or take notes to answer the questions.

1. Why does Andy multitask while he does his homework?
2. In the chart on page 63, fill in statistics and ideas about the uses of digital devices that each source provides. The first one is done as an example.

Source	Information
(¶2) Pew Internet and American Life Project	*87% of American teens use Internet 50% were online daily (2005)*
(¶3) Teenage Research Unlimited	
(¶3–¶5) Kaiser Study	
(¶6–¶8) David E. Meyer	
(¶10–¶11) Ned Hallowell	

3. What are some of the solutions suggested for gaining control if a person overuses or abuses technology?

Vocabulary Building

Read the underlined word or expression in its context and match it with the correct meaning. Use a dictionary if necessary.

_____ 1. It's likely that you and your friends understand the kind of multitasking that Andy <u>engages in</u> quite well. (¶2)

_____ 2. . . . there's something about computers with high-speed connections that causes <u>obsessive</u> multitasking. (¶5)

_____ 3. Many people . . . think that multitasking is the best way to <u>accomplish</u> a lot in a small amount of time. (¶6)

_____ 4. What your brain does instead is <u>prioritize</u> tasks. (¶8)

_____ 5. But it takes a lot of mental energy for your brain to keep <u>reorienting</u> itself back to each task. . . . (¶8)

_____ 6. . . . the <u>competing</u> tasks can't be too complicated. (¶9)

_____ 7. Are Andy and the thousands of teens like him <u>doomed</u> to a life chained to technology? (¶13)

_____ 8. . . . a sign that you're a tech <u>addict</u>. (¶13)

a. put in order of importance with most important first

b. someone who cannot stop a harmful habit

c. two or more things fighting for attention

d. condemned, certain to be destroyed by

e. do successfully

f. directing attention again

g. takes part in

h. constant (not able to stop)

Synonyms

Read the underlined word or expression in its context. Circle the two choices that are similar in meaning in this context. Use a dictionary if necessary.

1. Andy says he multitasks because otherwise he finds it hard to <u>concentrate</u>. (¶1)

   a. daydream   b. focus   c. pay attention

2. He hates to be out of touch with his <u>friends</u>. (¶1)

   a. buddies   b. siblings   c. pals

3. . . . your brain cannot process more than one <u>complex</u> task at a time. . . . (¶7)

   a. anxious   b. complicated   c. difficult

4. . . . you can't be talking about two different things <u>simultaneously</u>. (¶7)

   a. at the same time   b. at once   c. repeatedly

5. . . . spending all that time with your <u>gadgets</u> takes away from face-to-face time with actual humans. (¶11)

   a. devices   b. tasks   c. gizmos

6. . . . multitasking <u>keeps him from</u> hanging out with his friends in person. . . . (¶12)

   a. prepares him for   b. prevents him from   c. stops him from

7. Don't try to <u>keep in touch with</u> all of them (your MySpace friends) like BFFs. (¶13)

   a. dream about   b. be in contact with   c. stay in touch with

8. . . . teens can <u>break free from</u> their gadgets. (¶14)

   a. liberate themselves from   b. spend time with   c. separate from

9. It's <u>amazing</u> how much more time I have to see friends and go to basketball games. (¶14)

   a. astonishing   b. funny   c. surprising

Vocabulary Review

Complete the following statements about the reading selection with the correct word or expression from the list below. Use each word or expression only once.

accomplish	devices	prioritize
addicts	efficiently	reorient
complex	keep in touch	simultaneously

1. A lot of young people have access to numerous digital _____. They think they can _____ with friends, listen to music, watch TV shows, and do their homework all at the same time.

2. But the human brain can only multitask with simple tasks; it cannot handle two _____ tasks at once.

3. Every time you switch from one task to another, your brain has to

    _____ itself, which is time consuming.

4. You _____ less when you try to do several complicated

    tasks _____.

5. Multitasking means you work less _____, so your work

    takes much longer.

6. Multitasking _____—that is, people who overuse their

    gadgets—need to _____ tasks, so they can both do well in

    school and have time to hang out with their friends.

TEXT ANALYSIS

Headings

There are four headings in this article. What is each section about? Why do you think the author used the headings she did? Write a brief explanation for each one.

1. By the Numbers _____

2. Brain Drain _____

3. Make It Simple _____

4. Gaining Control _____

RESPONDING TO READING

Discuss these questions.

1. What do you think the author's opinion of multitasking is? Is she for it, against it, or does she have a balanced view? Do you agree with her or not? Why?

2. Would you like to increase or decrease the time you spend using technology? Explain. If you would like to decrease the time you spend using technology, would you follow the advice given in the last section, Gaining Control? Why or why not?

3. If you have "friends" through social networking pages, what kind of friends are they? Are they close friends that you regularly spend face-to-face time with? If not, how are they different?

"In the Blink of an Eye" was published in the *Lake Highlands Advocate* magazine in May 2004. The *Lake Highlands Advocate* is a local magazine for residents of Lake Highlands, Texas. The article was republished at the website of the North Texas PC Users Group (NTPCUG).

BEFORE YOU READ

Thinking about the Topic

Discuss these questions.

1. What are some of the problems that blind and visually impaired people have?
2. What are some things that help make their lives easier?
3. How can modern technology help them?

Previewing

Read the title and first two paragraphs, and answer the questions.

1. When did Robert Langford become blind?
2. How did blindness affect his life?

Before you read, turn to Comprehension Check, First Reading, on page 68. Your purpose for the first reading is to answer those questions.

READ

In the Blink of an Eye *By Becky Vaugh*

Robert Langford says computer technology helped him do things he hadn't done in more than 50 years. He now makes that technology available to blind persons around the world.

tragic
a. very good, wonderful
b. very bad, awful

drastically
a. in a small way
b. in a big way

1   On a Halloween night almost 60 years ago, 15-year-old Robert Langford was blinded as the result of a **tragic** Halloween night incident. That did not stop him from finishing high school, college, and earning a Ph.D. Over the years Langford led a fairly normal life: married, had children, and a career, but he was still dependent on other people for many things.

2   About 12 years ago, after he retired, his life changed. With the help of **drastically** improving technology, Langford's world opened up, allowing him to do the things most of us take for granted. Using a computer and voice synthesizer that told him everything that appeared on the monitor, he was able to start using the Internet, e-mail, word processors and other applications.

3   "For most of our lives, those of us who are totally blind have had to depend on someone else to do almost everything for us," he says. "And here I was, being able to read, write, keep records, and do things on a computer I hadn't done for myself since I was 15," he says.

4   Langford had already founded the Texas Center for the Physically Impaired (TCPI), a nonprofit group that helps handicapped people[1] find services and resources, and was operating it from his Lake Highlands home. Realizing he could

---

[1] **handicapped people** *an outdated term used for people with a disability*

equip them with
a. put in
b. sell them

help others achieve the same autonomy he had gained, he soon started refurbishing computers for other visually-impaired people.

5   He began by soliciting businesses and individuals for donated computers, then recruited volunteers from North Texas PC Users Group (NTPCUG) to refurbish and **equip them with** voice-synthesized software for the totally blind and text-enlarging software for the partially blind.

6   It didn't take long for news about the life-changing computers to spread.

7   "All of a sudden, people were deciding this was just exactly what they needed," he says. "The telephone was ringing 20, 30, 40 times a day."

8   Three years ago, TCPI was sending out about 100 computers a year. Langford says they're now up to roughly 400 a year, with more than 1,250 computers shipped to date.

9   "We had never dreamed it would come to this," he says. "I thought two years ago we had saturated the market. But people keep asking, and we keep sending computers out."

10   For just a $100 donation to help defray the costs for shipping, packaging, and parts, recipients receive a turnkey[2] computer system suited to their needs. They also receive audiocassettes and training materials that Langford prepares, teaching them how to do everything from turning the computer on to moving through the various programs and applications.

tremendous miracle
a. something very
   wonderful
b. a big problem

11   "When you're blind, learning how to use a computer is a lot of work," Langford says. "It takes real dedication, and some give up. But for those like me who put the effort and time into it, it's a **tremendous miracle.**"

12   Of course, he isn't able to do it all himself, and he's quick to give credit to his wife Doris, the people of TPCI and NTPCUG volunteers. Lake Highlands resident Gil Brand is one of those volunteers, spending at least two days a week on the project.

incredible
a. dishonest
b. extremely good

13   Langford is "just an **incredible** person," Brand says. "He's a ball of energy. He coordinates the receipt of donated computers, does the advertising, handles the requests and screens them, then we put them together and send them out."

14   Most of the computers are sent to people in the United States, but Langford and his volunteers are willing to help anyone, anywhere. They helped start a computer service for the blind in Chile a few years ago, after a woman there contacted them seeking help for her grandson. Langford and his wife even traveled to Chile for the dedication, which turned into a huge community event.

15   Word has traveled to Peru where there are now similar computer centers, and to other parts of the world. They've shipped computers to Sierra Leone, Romania, and Nigeria, and they hope to send more into Kenya, Honduras, and Nicaragua.

16   A lot to handle, but Langford shows no signs of slowing down.

mischief
a. trouble
b. the hospital

17   "I spend 6 to 10 hours a day on the computer or on the phone," he says. "I start at 6 or so every morning, and by the time I do all my e-mail, pay bills and keep records, then the telephone starts ringing. It gives me a tremendous amount of satisfaction. And it keeps me out of **mischief.**

boring
a. exciting
b. dull, uninteresting

18   "So many retired people find life **boring,** but I certainly don't. Every day I just can't wait to get started."

---

[2]**turnkey** *a product that can be used with no additional work required by the buyer; it includes hardware and software*

First Reading

Answer these questions.

1. How have computers helped Robert Langford?
2. How is he helping other blind and visually impaired people?

Second Reading

Read the selection again. Mark the statements *T* (true) or *F* (false). Write the paragraph number(s) where you found evidence for each answer.

1. T   F   Langford started using computers early in his life.   ¶ ___

2. T   F   TCPI is a nonprofit organization.   ¶ ___

3. T   F   Langford works alone at TCPI.   ¶ ___

4. T   F   He buys old computers and fixes them for blind people
to use.   ¶ ___

5. T   F   He distributes computers to blind and visually impaired people only
in the United States.   ¶ ___

6. T   F   There is a continuing demand for the refurbished, turnkey computer
systems TCPI prepares.   ¶ ___

Vocabulary Building: Synonyms

**Read the underlined word or expression in its context. Circle the two choices
that are similar in meaning in this context. Use a dictionary if necessary.**

1. . . . Robert Langford was blinded as the result of a tragic Halloween night
<u>incident</u>. (¶1)

    a. event   b. occurrence   c. party

2. . . . Langford's world opened up, allowing him to do the things most of us
<u>take for granted</u>. (¶2)

    a. accept as a fact of life   b. assume without questioning   c. hate to do

3. Realizing he could further help others achieve the same <u>autonomy</u> he had
gained . . . (¶4)

    a. independence   b. self-sufficiency   c. wealth

4. . . . he soon started <u>refurbishing</u> computers for other visually-impaired
people. (¶4)

    a. buying   b. fixing   c. renewing

5. He began by <u>soliciting</u> businesses and individuals <u>for</u> donated
computers. . . . (¶5)

    a. asking for   b. improving   c. requesting

6. . . . for <u>donated</u> computers . . . (¶5)

    a. contributed   b. given (for free)   c. new

7. . . . then <u>recruited</u> volunteers . . . (¶5)

    a. found   b. got   c. trained

8. I thought two years ago we had <u>saturated the market</u>. (¶9)

    a. created the demand   b. met the demand   c. satisfied the demand

9. . . . to help <u>defray</u> the costs . . . (¶10)

    a. increase   b. pay   c. offset

10. . . . <u>recipients</u> receive a turnkey computer system suited to their needs. (¶10)

    a. people who donate   b. people who get   c. people who receive

11. It (for a blind person to learn to use a computer) takes real <u>dedication</u>, and some give up. (¶11)

    a. concentration and commitment

    b. money and office space

    c. work and effort

12. He <u>coordinates</u> the receipt of donated computers, does the advertising, handles the requests, and screens them. . . . (¶13)

    a. finishes   b. organizes   c. oversees

Vocabulary Review

Complete the following statements about the reading selection with the correct word or expression from the list below. Use each word or expression only once.

autonomy	defray	equip	recipient
coordinates	donate	incredible	refurbish

1. Blind since the age of 15, Robert Langford is a(an) _____ person.

2. He _____ a program that asks people to _____ computers.

3. Volunteers then _____ the computers and _____ them with the software needed so that blind people can enjoy the same benefits of technology as people who can see.

4. The _____ pays $100 to help _____ the costs, a small price to pay for the _____ this specially equipped computer gives them.

Acronyms

In the strictest definition, an acronym is a word formed from the first letters of other words and pronounced as a single word.

> **Examples:** *scuba* diving (self-contained underwater breathing apparatus)
> NASA (National Aeronautics and Space Administration)

Using a broader definition, the letters may be pronounced separately.

> **Example:** UN (United Nations)

In formal writing, it is customary to use the individual words the first time, followed by the acronym in parentheses.

> **Example:** Texas Center for the Physically Impaired (TCPI)

Acronyms are common in company and organization names and therefore are often seen in website addresses, such as www.ntpcug.org, the site at which this article was published online.

> *Tip: To find out what acronyms stand for, enter the following into an Internet search engine: World Wide Web Acronym and Abbreviation Server*

Answer these questions. Write your answers on the lines.

1. What do these common acronyms stand for? You may find more than one answer for some.

    a. PC _____

    b. WWW _____

    c. FAQ _____

    d. IM _____

    e. PDF file _____

    f. FYI _____

    g. RSVP (French sentence, but common in English) _____

    h. ABC, BBC, CBS, CNN, NBC _____

    _____

2. What other acronyms do you use regularly? _____

RESPONDING TO READING

Discuss these questions.

1. What kinds of hardware and software are necessary to enable blind people to use computers? Google the American Foundation for the Blind. On their website, click on Technology and read the section. Talk to your classmates about what you learned.

2. What other kinds of technology help the blind, hearing impaired, and people with other disabilities?

3. What kinds of technology might be invented in the future to help people with disabilities?

4. What are other uses of technology that help people in other areas, such as medicine and sports?

CHAPTER 11

ABOUT THE READING

"Advertisers Try New Ways to Get into Your Head" was a feature news story on *ABC World News* with Charles Gibson in December 2006. ABC News Internet Ventures adapted the original news broadcast for the Internet version that appears here.

BEFORE YOU READ

Thinking about the Topic

Discuss these questions.

1. In addition to personal uses, where else do you see technology being used? What type of technology is it, and for what purposes is it used?
2. How is high technology used in advertising? What are some uses of technology that people may consider *an invasion of privacy*—in other words, interfering in their private lives?

Previewing

Read the title and the subhead, and answer the questions.

1. What does *get into your head* mean?
2. *Marketers* are people who try to sell things through carefully planned advertising. What do you think this article is going to tell us about what marketers are doing?

Before you read, turn to Comprehension Check, First Reading, on page 72. Your purpose for the first reading is to be able to answer those questions.

READ

Advertisers Try New Ways to Get into Your Head *By Gigi Stone*

Technologies Allow Marketers to Influence Buying Strategies Like Never Before

1   If you're like most Americans, by the time you get to work in the morning, marketers have tried to sell you something more than 200 times.

2   Ads[1] are now in places they've never been before—from subway turnstiles[2] to the floors of parking garages, and from bathroom stalls to video games.

3   But advertising experts say the more **conventional** ad barrage isn't capturing consumers' attention.

4   "The fact that consumers are being bombarded by so many messages basically means that they start to tune it out," said Jonah Blum, editor of *Advertising Age* Magazine. "It all becomes no more than white noise."[3]

(continued)

conventional
a. normal, usual
b. expensive

---

[1]**ads** *short for* advertisements

[2]**subway turnstile**

[3]**white noise** *meaningless noise that prevents people from getting a message*

Chapter 11 **71**

5   Cutting through the white noise is all about finding a better way to identify customers and what they want.

6   Advertisers' newest tactics include plasma screens that are being placed in shopping malls across the country. The screens analyze shoppers' faces to determine if they're male or female and then put up a different ad based on gender. They can even determine age and ethnicity.

7   Research shows such marketing can lift sales more than 300 percent, according to David Polinchock, the founder and chairman of Brand Experience Lab.

8   "The more that you can **target** an ad specifically to what a person is looking for, what they might need, and who they are, the better you have a chance to connect with those people," Polinchock explained.

NEW TECHNOLOGIES REVEAL CONSUMERS' THOUGHT PROCESS

9   The grocery giant Stop & Shop has tried a new gadget at selected stores. Customers swipe a card[4] and a shopping list **pops up** based on items the person has bought before, along with suggestions for new products to buy.

10   For companies, it's valuable information about buyers' habits. The question is, how will the information be used?

11   "If your HMO[5] had a record of your nutritional health profile, they could use that info[6] to raise your **rates**," said Katherine Albrecht, a consumer privacy expert and the founder and director of CASPIAN, Consumers Against Supermarket Privacy Invasion and Numbering, a national consumer organization created in 1999 to educate people about shopper surveillance.

12   Albrecht said supermarket cards and retail surveillance devices are merely the opening volley of the marketers' **monitoring** of consumers.

13   Retailers are tracking their habits in other ways too. In fact, the next time you go shoe shopping, consider this: New technology may be monitoring not just which sneaker you pick up, but also how long you hold it.

14   The point? To better understand the psychology of the consumer, or put more simply, to get inside your brain.

___

[4]**swipe a card** *to put a card through an electronic device that reads it*
[5]**HMO** *health management organization*
[6]**info** *short for* information

target
a. aim
b. remove

pops up
a. breaks
b. appears

rates
a. amount you pay
b. speed

monitoring
a. helping
b. watching, observing

COMPREHENSION CHECK

First Reading

Circle the letter of the correct answer.

1. Why is the usual way of advertising less effective nowadays?

   a. There are so many ads that people don't pay attention to them.

   b. There are not enough ads to get people's attention.

   c. The ads are so confusing that people don't understand them.

2. What type of advertising does the writer object to most?

   a. using attractive computer graphics

   b. putting ads on TV screens in stores

   c. directing ads at specific people

Second Reading

Read the selection again, and highlight or take notes to answer the questions.

1. According to this article, where do people see and hear advertisements?

   _____

2. What are two or three examples given in this selection of the efforts by marketers to individualize ads? _____

   _____

3. What indication is there that this type of advertising is successful?

   _____

4. Why would an HMO be interested in the food you buy, your "nutritional health profile"? _____

5. What does the last sentence suggest about the writer's opinion of these uses of this technology? _____

   _____

VOCABULARY

Vocabulary Building

Read the underlined word or expression in its context and match it with the correct meaning. Use a dictionary if necessary.

___ 1. . . . consumers are being <u>bombarded</u> by so many messages. . . . (¶4)

___ 2. . . . they start to <u>tune it out.</u> . . . (¶4)

___ 3. Advertisers' newest <u>tactics</u> include plasma screens that are being placed in shopping malls across the country. (¶6)

___ 4. . . . put up a different ad based on <u>gender</u>. (¶6)

___ 5. They can even determine age and <u>ethnicity</u>. (¶6)

___ 6. . . . Katherine Albrecht, . . . the founder and director of CASPIAN, Consumers Against Supermarket <u>Privacy Invasion</u> and Numbering . . . (¶11)

___ 7. . . . to educate people about shopper <u>surveillance</u>. (¶11)

___ 8. <u>Retailers</u> are tracking their habits in other ways too. (¶13)

a. whether male or female

b. people who sell directly to consumers

c. pay no attention to it

d. careful watching or tracking, monitoring

e. attacked

f. planned actions, strategies

g. race, nation, or tribe

h. trying to find out about someone's personal life in a way that is improper and perhaps illegal

Vocabulary Review

Complete the following statements about the reading selection with the correct word or expression from the list below. Use each word or expression only once.

bombarded   rates   target

gender   tactic   tune them out

invasion of privacy

1. Consumers are constantly _____ with so many ads that instead of listening to them many people _____.

2. To try to make people pay attention, marketers are using new technology to _____ individuals.

3. One _____ they use is to monitor our shopping behavior. They also use technology to recognize our _____, age, and ethnicity to show us ads for things they think we would like to buy.

4. Some consumers consider this a serious _____. How would you feel, for example, if your health insurance company found out you were buying a lot of junk food and raised your medical insurance _____?

TEXT ANALYSIS   *Maintaining a Metaphor*

Good writers choose their words carefully; sometimes they choose words to create a metaphor. This writer chose words related to a military attack; therefore the metaphor is war. Read the definitions of some of the words she chose.

barrage (¶3) *n.* the continuous shooting of guns

capture (¶3) *v.* to catch someone in order to keep him/her as a prisoner; to take control, often by using force

bombard (¶4) *v.* to attack with guns or bombs

tactic(s) (¶6) *n.* the way the military uses its armies, weapons, etc. in order to win a battle

target (¶8) *v.* to deliberately attack someone or something, aim at

surveillance (¶11) *n.* the act of carefully watching a particular person or place (military or police surveillance)

the opening volley (¶12) *n.* the first round of shooting arrows or guns

The writer could have expressed her ideas in other ways, as shown in the right column of the chart below. Study the chart and answer the questions that follow.

The Writer Expressed the Idea This Way:	The Writer Could Have Written:
. . . the more conventional ad <u>barrage</u> isn't <u>capturing</u> consumers' attention. (¶3)	. . . the more conventional ads are not getting consumers' attention.
. . . consumers are being <u>bombarded</u> by so many messages. . . . (¶4)	. . . consumers are receiving so many messages. . . .
Advertisers' newest <u>tactics</u> include . . . (¶6)	Advertisers' newest ways of advertising include . . .
. . . <u>target</u> an ad specifically to what a person is looking for . . . (¶8)	. . . create an ad for a specific audience . . .
. . . retail <u>surveillance</u> devices are merely <u>the opening volley</u> of the marketers' monitoring of consumers. (¶12)	. . . retail tracking devices are only the beginning of the marketers' monitoring of consumers.

1. Who is the attacker? _____
2. Who is being attacked? _____
3. What is the weapon? _____
4. How would the selection be different if the writer had chosen the words in the right column? _____

_____

RESPONDING TO READING

Discuss these questions.

1. What is the writer's message? Consider the military metaphor, the title, and the last sentence. How does the writer create unity in this selection?

2. What is your reaction to the ads that you encounter? Do you pay attention to them? Do they influence what you buy?

3. This article presents one use of technology that many people think is an invasion of privacy. What other uses of technology do you know about that people might object to?

CHAPTER 12

ABOUT THE READING

This short story by the British writer Jim Crace (1946–) is from *Flash Fiction Forward*, a collection of very short stories. It was originally published in 2001 in *The Devil's Larder,* a book of sixty-four short fiction pieces by Crace about food; this one is number 21.

BEFORE YOU READ

Thinking about the Topic

Discuss these questions.

1. What type of information does your *purchases*, the things you buy, reveal about you?
2. How might this information be used?

Before you read, turn to Comprehension Check, First Reading, on page 77. Your purpose for the first reading is to be able to answer those questions.

READ

21 *By Jim Crace*

1 A youngish man, a trifle overweight, too anxious for his age, completed his circuit of the supermarket shelves and cabinets and stood in line, ashamed as usual.

2 He arranged his purchases on the checkout belt and waited, with his eyes fixed on the street beyond the shop window, while the woman at the till[1] scanned all the bar codes on his medicines, his vitamins, his air freshener, his toilet tissue, his frozen Meals for One, his tins,[2] his magazines, his beer, and his deodorant, his bread, bananas, milk, his fat-free yogurt, his jar of decaf,[3] and his treats: today, some roasted chicken legs, some grapes, a block of chocolate, and two croissants.[4] He rubbed his thumb along the embossed numbers of his credit card while each item triggered a **trill** of recognition from the till.

3 The till's computer recognized the young man's Distinctive Shopping Fingerprint as well, the usual ratio of fat to starch, the familiar selection of canned food, the recent and increasing range of health supplements, the unique combination of monthly magazines. The pattern of the shopping identified the customer. Even before the woman at the till had swiped the credit card, the computer had lined up the young man's details—his list of purchases for the previous seven months, his credit rating, his Customer Loyalty score. It knew broadly who he was and how he lived. It could deduce what his modest rooms above the travel shop were like, how stale they were, how flowerless, how functional, how **crying out for** change. Here was the man whose cat had died or run away three months ago. No cat food purchased since that time. Here was the customer who had not left the neighborhood for more than seven days in living, byte-sized memory. Last spring, he'd tried and failed to cut down on patisseries[5] and sugar. Today, for once, he had resisted his usual impulse purchase of a packet of cheroots.[6]

trill
a. sound
b. effort

crying out for
a. in need of
b. saddened by

---

[1]**till** *cash register (British English)*
[2]**tins** *metal cans (British English)*
[3]**decaf** *decaffeinated coffee, without caffeine (caffeine is a stimulant that makes you feel more awake)*

[4]**croissants** *French rolls shaped in a curve, made with a lot of butter*
[5]**patisseries** *French for pastries (e.g., small sweet cakes)*
[6]**cheroots** *cigars*

Computer screened a message on the woman's till: Cheroots . . . Cheroots . . . it said. Remind the customer he has not purchased cereals or cheese or vegetables this month. Remind him of our *special offers*: 12 cans of lager for the price of 10. Buy one bottle of our Boulevard liqueur and get a second free. Remind him that time is passing more quickly than he thinks—his washing powder should be used by now, as should the contraceptives that he bought two years ago. He must need basics, such as rice and pasta, soap, toothpaste, flour, oil, and condiments[7]. Inform him of our Retail Schemes[8] and that we open now on Sunday afternoons. Advise him that he ought to do more cooking for himself. He ought to tidy up and clean the bathroom tiles with our new lemon whitener. He ought to start afresh. Suggest to him he tour our shelves again. **At once.** For what we choose is what we are. He should not miss this second opportunity to re-create himself with food.

at once
a. at the same time
b. immediately, right now

---

[7]**condiments** *sauces used with food to add flavor or taste (e.g., ketchup, mustard)*

[8]**Retail Schemes** *special offers promoting certain products*

COMPREHENSION CHECK

First Reading

Answer these questions.

1. What can you infer about how well the man eats?
2. Do you think he has a family, or do you think he lives alone? How do you know?

Second Reading

A. Read the selection again. Mark the statement *R* (reasonable) or *U* (unreasonable) based on the information in the selection. Find evidence that supports your answers and write it on the lines.

1. R U The man in the story is a relaxed person.

   _____

2. R U He is a vegetarian.

   _____

3. R U He usually cooks meals from scratch—that is, with fresh ingredients, not prepared meals.

   _____

4. R U He doesn't travel much.

   _____

5. R U He is not very pleasant with the cashier.

   _____

6. R U In some ways he thinks about his health.

   _____

7. R U He is a good housekeeper.

   _____

8. R U He is a good athlete.

   _____

B. List the advice that the store's computer system gives him.

_____

_____

VOCABULARY

Vocabulary Building: Synonyms

Read the underlined word or expression in its context. Circle the two choices that are similar in meaning in this context. Use a dictionary if necessary.

1. A youngish man . . . too <u>anxious</u> for his age . . . (¶1)

   a. nervous   b. relaxed   c. worried

2. . . . stood in line, <u>ashamed</u> as usual. (¶1)

   a. embarrassed   b. proud   c. uncomfortable

3. He arranged his <u>purchases</u> on the checkout belt. . . . (¶2)

   a. items you buy   b. items you pay for   c. items you sell

4. . . . each item <u>triggered</u> a trill of recognition from the till. (¶2)

   a. caused   b. initiated   c. shot

5. . . . the usual <u>ratio</u> of fat to starch . . . (¶3)

   a. proportion   b. reason   c. relative amount

6. . . . increasing <u>range</u> of health supplements . . . (¶3)

   a. assortment   b. place   c. variety

7. . . . the <u>unique</u> combination of monthly magazines. (¶3)

   a. common   b. particular   c. one-of-a-kind

8. It could <u>deduce</u> what his modest rooms above the travel shop were like. . . . (¶3)

   a. destroy   b. infer   c. guess

9. . . . he'd tried and failed to <u>cut down on</u> patisseries and sugar. (¶3)

   a. eat less   b. make his own   c. reduce the amount of

10. . . . he had <u>resisted</u> his usual impulse purchase. . . . (¶3)

    a. accepted   b. fought against   c. refused to give in to

11. He ought to <u>tidy up</u> and clean the bathroom tiles. . . . (¶4)

    a. move away   b. do some housekeeping   c. put things away

Vocabulary Review

Complete the following statements about the reading selection with the correct word or expression from the list below. Use each word or expression only once.

cut down on	purchases	trigger
deduce	range	unique

1. When you go shopping, the store's computer system identifies you and keeps a record of all your _____.

2. Knowing the whole _____ of products you buy and how often you buy them, it can _____ a lot of things about your personal life.

3. It knows what you eat, how you live, and what you are trying to _____.

4. Your profile can then _____ the use of ads that are especially targeted at you.

5. You may be a _____ individual, but without knowing you personally, the system knows a lot about you.

TEXT ANALYSIS

British English

Jim Crace, the author of this story, is British. British English differs slightly from American English. Match the British vocabulary item on the left with the equivalent American vocabulary on the right.

___ 1. till (¶2)   a. cans
___ 2. tins (¶2)   b. special offers
___ 3. washing powder (¶4) c. put things away
___ 4. retail schemes (¶4) d. cash register
___ 5. tidy up (¶4)   e. laundry detergent

Creating an Effect with Few Words

Flash fiction is very short; this story is just under 500 words, yet the author paints a picture of an individual as well as an aspect of the society he lives in. The way the author tells this story without any comment or explanation creates an effect. Put a check (✓) on the lines next to the effects that are created by this style of writing. Discuss your answers with a partner.

___ 1. It makes the picture of the man more emotional and subjective.

___ 2. It makes the picture of the man more objective and distant.

___ 3. The author is like a surveillance camera.

___ 4. It makes the man seem more likable.

___ 5. The reader can see that the man is concerned about the computer invading his privacy.

RESPONDING TO READING

Discuss these questions.

1. What title would you give this story?

2. How is this story an example of the type of advertising described in Chapter 11? Do you think the man finds it an invasion of his privacy? Explain.

3. What could Jim Crace be telling us with regard to individuals and the technology that surrounds us?

Extending Your Vocabulary

Word Families

Study the chart below to learn other forms of some of the words in this unit. If there is a box with a dash, either there is no word to fill it or the word is missing because it is not one you need to know now.

	NOUNS	VERBS	ADJECTIVES	ADVERBS
1.	accomplishment	accomplish	—	—
2.	addict addiction	—	addictive addicted	—
3.	anxiety	—	anxious	anxiously
4.	efficiency inefficiency	—	efficient inefficient	efficiently inefficiently
5.	invasion	invade	invasive	—
6.	obsession	obsess	obsessive	obsessively
7.	priority	prioritize	—	—
8.	recipient	receive	—	—
9.	sequence	sequence	sequential	sequentially
10.	—	—	simultaneous	simultaneously

For each item below, look at the row in the chart above with the same number. Choose the word that correctly completes each sentence. Be sure it is in the correct form.

1. Becoming fluent in a second language is not easy; it's quite an _____.

2. For some people surfing the Internet is _____; they spend hours online.

3. Aida was waiting _____ to hear the election results.

4. Multitasking is not an _____ use of time.

5. In the movie, Martians _____ Earth and destroy our civilization.

6. Robert checks his e-mail _____. I wonder how he has time for anything else. He clearly has an _____ with keeping in touch with his friends.

7. If you really want to do something, you have to make it a _____.

8. The _____ of the award gets a trophy and also

   _____ $500 in cash.

9. Let's get the events of this story in the right _____. What

   happened first?

10. Emilio is completely bilingual in Spanish and English. He is studying

    _____ translation.

Collocations

One way to extend your vocabulary is to learn new collocations for words. Using correct collocations makes you sound more like a native speaker.

capture (v.)	**capture** attention, criminals, (the) enemy, (the) imagination, a (large) share of the market
rate(s) (n.)	birth, interest, shipping, tax, vacancy **rates** lower, reduce, raise **rates**
recruit (v.)	**recruit** forces, new members, soldiers, staff, volunteers, workers
trigger (v.)	**trigger** a protest, a revolt, an allergic reaction, an economic depression, a response, a revival, an increase in prices/interest rates/spending
surveillance (n.)	**surveillance** cameras, monitors, systems consumer, military, retail **surveillance** under **surveillance**

Complete the sentences below with appropriate collocations. Look at the chart above for help. There may be more than one correct collocation for some sentences.

1. *Harry Potter* has captured _____ of a whole generation.

2. The advertising campaign was a success, and they captured

   _____.

3. In places where women have more education, the _____

   rate is lower.

4. If banks can _____ rates on loans, more people will be able

   to borrow money.

5. It isn't always easy to recruit _____ for the army.

6. We're a nonprofit organization; we have to recruit _____.

7. Bee stings trigger _____ in some people, which can be very

   dangerous.

8. Price increases sometimes trigger _____.

(continued)

9. The police have several suspects _____ surveillance; they were all at the scene of the crime.

10. There are surveillance _____ in many places in order to increase security.

WRITING

Choose one of the suggestions for writing below. Talk about what you plan to write with a classmate who chose the same topic. Then follow the instructions for writing.

1. Write a paragraph or two about the way you use or would like to use technology.

2. If a computer analyzed what you buy, what would it find out about you? Fill in the chart below and then answer the questions that follow.

What You Regularly Buy	How Often	What It Shows about You

   a. What could someone infer about you from what you buy?
   b. What products would stores urge you to buy?

3. Write a paragraph or two about personalized ads that might be aimed at you, for example, for shoes, athetic equipment, or books. How would you feel about being targeted in this way?

4. Write about unequal access to digital media in different parts of the world as shown in the graphs at the beginning of this unit. What problems might children have if they don't have access to computers early in their lives? What could be a solution to this problem? If you have access to the Internet, you might want to visit the sites of the Gates Foundation, One Laptop per Child, or the American Library Association.

Try to use some of the following vocabulary in writing about the topic you choose: *accomplish, addict, complex, conventional ads, cut down on, device, doomed to, efficient, gadgets, invasion of privacy, keep in touch with, obsessive, overuse, pops up, prioritize, purchases, surveillance, target, tune out.*

High Tech Glossary

applications software programs for users (e.g., word processors, spread sheets, voice synthesizers)

blog a Web log or journal kept on the Internet where the person maintaining the blog (the blogger) expresses his or her opinions and other people can comment

byte a measure of computer storage space; a byte is 8 bits or characters

browser a computer program for accessing and interacting with text, images, videos, music, and other information on the World Wide Web

digital media high tech sources of information such as the Internet, CDs (compact disks), DVDs (digital video disks), iPods®, and other MP3 players

download to bring files from the Internet to your computer

e-mail electronic mail using computers and the Internet

handheld device small computing equipment, also called mobile device, such as a cellular phone and PDA (personal digital assistant)

information age the present global economy, which has shifted from a focus on producing physical products to a focus on handling information

instant message (IM) real-time communication via the Internet using typed text, more like a conversation than e-mail

interface a means of communication between two things; for example, the keyboard is an interface between the computer user and the computer

Internet the World Wide Web, a network of interconnected computers allowing worldwide transfer of messages and information

log on to start computer use or get on to a network

log off to stop computer use or get off a network

monitor a computer screen

MP3 players and iPods devices for recording, storing, and playing digital media, such as audio books, music, podcasts, and videos

(be) online logged on to the Internet or other network

social networking pages (e.g., Facebook®, MySpace®) websites offering user-submitted personal profiles, blogs, photos, music, and videos for various purposes

text message to send a message via text messaging on a cell phone or other handheld device

upload to send files from your computer to the Internet

virtual in the environment of cyberspace, referring to life online

voice synthesizer a program or application that converts text-to-speech (TTS)

YouTube® a free video-sharing website that lets users upload, view, and share video clips

Looking for Love

Discuss

1. How do people find romantic partners?
2. What do people want from a long-term romantic relationship?
3. In what ways do people learn about each other before marriage?

Though pop singers may croon "I love you," lasting relationships depend more on "I like you."

Catherine Houck, *What Makes a Marriage Last*

"Students Think Love Conquers All" is an adaptation of a research report that appeared in the magazine *USA Today*.

BEFORE YOU READ

Thinking about the Topic

Discuss these questions.

1. The title of this article includes the expression "love conquers all," which means that love can solve all problems. Do you think love can solve all problems in a romantic relationship? Explain.
2. Do you think most people believe love conquers all? Think about men versus women and older people versus younger people.

Previewing

Read the title and the first paragraph of this selection, and answer the questions.

1. From the title alone, what do you think the researchers studied?
2. Who were the participants in the study?
3. What did the participants in the study believe?

Before you read, turn to Comprehension Check, First Reading, on page 86. Your purpose for the first reading is to be able to answer those questions.

READ

expected
a. didn't want to happen
b. thought was going to happen

single
a. married
b. not married

Students Think Love Conquers All *USA Today Staff*

1   When it comes to relationships, the honeymoon[1] never ends, at least not in the minds of college students who were part of a study to measure what they **expected** from their relationships. The researchers found that students believed their relationships would keep getting better and better over time.

2   "These kinds of expectations are like something you would find in a 1950s Doris Day–Rock Hudson[2] movie. But they are contrary to what research suggests about marital satisfaction," according to Andrew I. Schwebel, professor of psychology at Ohio State University. He says that such optimistic expectations can result in marital dissatisfaction later in life.

3   "Someone might think, for instance, 'Well, I'm not really happy with my partner right now, but since things are going to get better, I'll go ahead and marry him or her.'"

4   Schwebel and his student Bryce Sullivan studied 238 students ranging in age from 18 to 34. All were **single**, although more than a quarter were dating only one person and had discussed marriage with their partner.

(continued)

---

[1]**honeymoon** *a trip that a couple takes after their wedding; also refers to happiness in the first months of marriage*
[2]**Doris Day** and **Rock Hudson** *American actress and actor who appeared together in a number of romantic movies with happy endings in the 1950s*

average
a. special
b. typical

unrealistically
a. impossibly
b. a little

setting themselves
up for
a. asking for
b. trying to avoid

5   Each student was asked to complete a questionnaire about their expectations for four different stages of a relationship: casual dating, engagement, five years of marriage, and fifteen years of marriage. The students also were asked what they thought the **average** American's relationship would be like at these same stages.

6   Based on their answers, researchers could see that students felt their own relationships would be much better in the future than those of other couples. In some ways, Schwebel says, such beliefs can be helpful. "We want people to have positive expectations because this leads them to try harder. On the other hand, there's probably some cutoff point where their expectations are **unrealistically** high.

7   "For example," Sullivan suggests, "people who think they are never going to have any trouble in their marriage may be **setting themselves up for** disappointment. It would be much better if they realized that marriage can be tough, and they're going to have to work pretty hard to make it succeed."

COMPREHENSION CHECK

First Reading

Answer these questions.

1. What do students believe about their relationships?
2. Do the researchers agree with the students? Explain.

Second Reading

A. Read the selection again, and answer the questions.

1. Who did the study? _____

2. Where was the study done? _____

3. How many people participated in the study? _____

4. How old were the participants? _____

5. Were they married or single? _____

6. The researchers asked the students to respond to a questionnaire about their expectations for their relationships at four stages. What were the four stages?

   Stage 1: _____

   Stage 2: _____

   Stage 3: _____

   Stage 4: _____

7. In addition to asking about expectations about their own relationships at these four stages, they also asked the students what they thought the relationships of _____ would be like at these same stages.

B. Choose the best answer. Write the paragraph number(s) where you found evidence for each answer.

1. The students believe that the average person's relationship is ¶ _____

   a. better than their own.

   b. not as good as their own.

2. Which statement would Professor Schwebel agree with? ¶ _____

   a. When people think a bad relationship is going to get better, it usually will get better.

   b. A positive attitude, or optimism, leads to marital satisfaction.

   c. High expectations are good for a relationship but only within limits.

3. Which statement would Sullivan agree with? ¶ _____

   a. If you have high expectations for your marriage, it will succeed.

   b. Marriage is difficult, and it takes work to make it succeed.

VOCABULARY

Vocabulary Building

Read the underlined word or expression in its context. Choose the meaning that makes sense in this context. Use a dictionary if necessary.

1. But they (these kinds of expectations) are <u>contrary to</u> what research suggests. . . . (¶2)

   a. exactly   b. similar to   c. the opposite of

2. . . . what research suggests about <u>marital satisfaction</u> . . . (¶2)

   a. divorce   b. happiness in marriage   c. marital problems

3. . . . such <u>optimistic</u> expectations can result in marital dissatisfaction later in life. (¶2)

   a. negative   b. positive   c. realistic

4. Each student was asked to complete a <u>questionnaire</u> about their expectations. . . . (¶5)

   a. application for an online dating service   b. set of questions to collect information   c. test

5. . . . for four different stages of a relationship: <u>casual</u> dating . . . (¶5)

   a. arranged, planned   b. not serious, informal   c. serious, formal

6. . . . casual dating, <u>engagement</u>, five years of marriage . . . (¶5)

   a. agreement to marry   b. anniversary   c. personal plans

(continued)

7. We want people to have positive expectations because this <u>leads</u> them <u>to</u> try harder. (¶6)

    a. causes   b. forces   c. requires

8. . . . there's probably some <u>cutoff point</u> where their expectations are unrealistically high. (¶6)

    a. average   b. contribution   c. limit

9. It would be much better if they realized that marriage can be <u>tough</u>. . . . (¶7)

    a. difficult   b. easy   c. fun

Vocabulary Review

Complete the following statements about the reading selection with the correct word or expression from the list below. Use each word or expression only once.

average	lead to	optimistic
expectations	marital satisfaction	tough

1. The researchers found that the college students they studied are unrealistically _____ about their relationships.

2. The subjects in this study have higher _____ for themselves than for the _____ American couple.

3. Their positive attitude can be good, up to a point, but it can _____ dissatisfaction later in life.

4. Couples should realize that marriage can be _____ and that spouses have to work hard to achieve long-term _____.

TEXT ANALYSIS   *Understanding Connections*

> Understanding how the ideas in writing are connected will help your comprehension. Using words that refer to something else in the text (the referent) is one way to make connections that hold the text together without too much repetition.

Show what the underlined words refer or connect to by answering the question below each item. Go back to the reading selection for the context. The first one has been done for you.

1. <u>These kinds of expectations</u> . . . (¶2)

    What expectations are the authors referring to?

    They are referring to the students' expectations that their relationships will keep getting better and better (¶1).

2. But <u>they</u> are contrary to what research suggests. . . . (¶2)

What does *they* refer to?

_____

3. <u>All</u> were single. . . . (¶4)

Who does *all* refer to?

_____

4. . . . students felt their own relationships would be much better in the future

than <u>those</u> of other couples. (¶6)

What does *those* refer to?

_____

5. In some ways, Schwebel says, <u>such beliefs</u> can be helpful. (¶6)

What does *such beliefs* refer to?

_____

**RESPONDING
TO READING**

Discuss these questions.

1. Why do you think people expect their own relationships to be better than other people's relationships?

2. Suppose your partner has different ideas from you in the following areas:

   - how to spend money
   - his or her attitude toward working
   - how many children to have
   - how clean the house should be
   - ways to spend leisure time
   - other areas you may think of: _____

   a. Which of these areas are more important than others?
   b. Is it reasonable to expect your partner to change in any of these areas? If so, which ones? Give your reasons.

ABOUT THE READING

This selection comes from *What Do You Care What Other People Think? Further Adventures of a Curious Character* by Richard P. Feynman (1918–1988) as told to Ralph Leighton. The book is a collection of autobiographical stories. Many of them are related to Feynman's work as a physicist and member of the presidential commission to investigate the accident that destroyed the space shuttle *Challenger* on January 28, 1986. This excerpt, however, is about dating in the 1930s. Feynman won the Nobel Prize for Physics in 1965.

BEFORE YOU READ

Thinking about the Topic

Discuss these questions.

1. What do you know about dating in the United States and in other countries where dating is a custom?
2. How do young people socialize in other cultures you are familiar with?

Previewing

Read the first two paragraphs of this selection, and answer the questions.

1. What do you think the rest of the reading will be about?
2. What importance, if any, could there be that the other guys are older than Feynman?

Before you read, turn to Comprehension Check, First Reading, on page 91. Your purpose for the first reading is to be able to answer those questions.

READ

Untitled *By Richard Feynman*

1   When I was a young fella,[1] about thirteen, I had somehow gotten in with a group of guys who were a little older than I was and more sophisticated. They knew a lot of different girls and would go out with them—often to the beach.

2   One time when we were at the beach, most of the guys had gone out on some jetty[2] with the girls. I was interested in a particular girl a little bit, and sort of thought out loud: "Gee, I think I'd like to take Barbara to the movies . . ."

3   That's all I had to say, and the guy next to me gets all excited. He runs out onto the rocks and finds her. He pushes her back, all the while saying in a loud voice, "Feynman has something he wants to say to you, Barbara!" It was most embarrassing.

4   Pretty soon the guys are all standing around me, saying, "Well, *say* it, Feynman!" So I invited her to the movies. It was my first date.

5   I went home and told my mother about it. She gave me all kinds of advice on how to do this and that. For example, if we take the bus, I'm supposed to get off the bus first, and offer Barbara my hand. Or if we have to walk in the street, I'm

---

[1]**fella** *informal pronunciation of* fellow, *which is a boy, man, or guy (male)*
[2]**jetty** *a wide wall built out into the water as protection against large waves*

the next generation
of women
a. older women
b. younger women

to be stuck
a. making progress
b. not making progress

complimented
a. said something nice
b. said something that
   is not nice, insulted

terrific
a. very good
b. very bad

supposed to walk on the outside[3]. She even told me what kinds of things to say. She was handing down a cultural tradition to me: the women teach their sons how to treat **the next generation of women** well.

6   After dinner, I get all slicked up[4] and go to Barbara's house to call for her. I'm nervous. She isn't ready, of course (it's always like that) so her family has me wait for her in the dining room, where they're eating with friends—a lot of people. They say things like, "Isn't he cute!" and all kinds of other stuff. I didn't feel cute. It was absolutely terrible!

7   I remember everything about the date. As we walked from her house to the new, little theater in town, we talked about playing the piano. I told her how, when I was younger, they made me learn piano for a while, but after six months I was still playing "Dance of the Daisies," and couldn't stand it anymore. You see, I was worried about being a sissy,[5] and **to be stuck** for weeks playing "Dance of the Daisies" was too much for me, so I quit. I was so sensitive about being a sissy that it even bothered me when my mother sent me to the market to buy some snacks called Peppermint Patties and Toasted Dainties.

8   We saw the movie, and I walked her back to her home. I **complimented** her on the nice, pretty gloves she was wearing. Then I said goodnight to her on the doorstep.

9   Barbara says to me, "Thank you for a very lovely evening."[6]

10   "You're welcome!" I answered. I felt **terrific**.

11   The next time I went out on a date—it was with a different girl—I say goodnight to her, and she says, "Thank you for a very lovely evening."

12   I didn't feel quite so terrific.

13   When I said goodnight to the third girl I took out, she's got her mouth open, ready to speak, and I say, "Thank you for a very lovely evening!"

14   She says, "Thank you—uh—Oh!—Yes—uh, I had a lovely evening, too, thank you!"

---

[3]**on the outside** *nearer to the traffic*
[4]**get all slicked up** *take special care in getting dressed up*
[5]**sissy** *a boy who looks or acts like a girl*
[6]**Thank you for a very lovely evening.** *When Feynman was young, girls routinely used this polite phrase at the end of a date.*

COMPREHENSION CHECK

First Reading

Answer these questions.

1. How did Feynman feel when his friends forced him to invite Barbara to the movies?
2. Did he enjoy his first date? How do you know?

Second Reading

A. Read the selection again. Mark the statements *T* (true) or *F* (false). Write the paragraph number(s) where you found evidence for each answer.

1. T F   Feynman's friends were boys who were the same age he was.   ¶ ____

2. T F   Feynman wasn't interested in asking Barbara out on a date.   ¶ ____

3. T F   His mother told him the correct things to do on a date.   ¶ ____

4. T F   He felt uncomfortable while he was waiting for Barbara at her house.   ¶ ____

5. T F Feynman worried that people might think he was a sissy. ¶ ___

6. T F Feynman felt good when Barbara thanked him for the evening. ¶ ___

7. T F Dating got easier for him on the next few dates. ¶ ___

B. This selection gives us ideas about dating customs in the United States when Feynman was growing up, in the 1930s. Fill in the chart below based on the information in the reading.

Things Boys Were Supposed to Do	Things Girls Were Supposed to Do
ask girls out	

VOCABULARY

Vocabulary Building: Synonyms

Read the underlined word or expression in its context. Circle the two choices that are similar in meaning in this context. Use a dictionary if necessary.

1. When I was . . . about thirteen, I had somehow gotten in with a group of <u>guys</u> who were a little older than I was. . . . (¶1)

   a. boys   b. fellas   c. girlfriends

2. . . . a little older than I was and more <u>sophisticated</u>. (¶1)

   a. athletic   b. experienced   c. grown up

3. It was most <u>embarrassing</u> (when they forced Feynman to invite Barbara to the movies). (¶3)

   a. awkward   b. humiliating   c. interesting

4. (My mother) gave me all kinds of <u>advice</u> on how to do this and that. (¶5)

   a. correction   b. recommendations   c. suggestions

5. . . . if we take the bus, I'm <u>supposed to</u> get off the bus first. . . . (¶5)

   a. am expected to   b. should   c. won't

6. She was handing down a cultural <u>tradition</u> to me. . . . (¶5)

   a. game   b. set of customs   c. way of doing things

7. (Barbara's parents and their friends) say things like, "Isn't he <u>cute</u>!" (¶6)

   a. attractive   b. nice looking   c. ugly

8. It was <u>absolutely</u> terrible! (¶6)

   a. completely   b. totally   c. usually

9. . . . after six months I was still playing "Dance of the Daisies," and I couldn't <u>stand it</u> anymore. (¶7)

   a. forget it   b. put up with it   c. tolerate it

10. . . . to be stuck for weeks playing "Dance of the Daisies" was too much for me, so I quit. (¶7)

   a. continued   b. gave up   c. stopped

11. I was so sensitive about being a sissy. . . . (¶7)

   a. concerned   b. strong   c. worried

12. . . . it even bothered me when my mother sent me to the market to buy some snacks called Peppermint Patties and Toasted Dainties. (¶7)

   a. interested   b. troubled   c. upset

Multiword Expressions

Read the underlined multiword expression in its context. Match it with the correct meaning. Use a dictionary if necessary.

____ 1. . . . I had somehow gotten in with a group of guys who were a little older than I was. . . . (¶1)

____ 2. They knew a lot of different girls, and would go out with them—often to the beach. (¶1)

____ 3. . . . I'm supposed to get off the bus first. . . . (¶5)

____ 4. She was handing down a cultural tradition to me. . . . (¶5)

____ 5. After dinner, I . . . go to Barbara's house to call for her. (¶6)

a. get her
b. become friends with
c. passing on, giving
d. go on dates with, take out
e. leave

Vocabulary Review

Complete the following statements about the reading selection with the correct word or expression from the list below. Use each word or expression only once.

| advice | cute | go out | sensitive |
| called for | embarrassing | guys | supposed to |

1. Some older, more sophisticated _____ forced Feynman to invite Barbara to the movies. It was a(n) _____ situation for him.

2. When he told his mother he was going to _____ with Barbara, she gave him some _____ about things boys are _____ do on a date.

3. When he _____ Barbara at her house, she wasn't ready.

4. He didn't like it when her parents and their friends said he was _____. He thought that word was not masculine, and he was very _____ about being seen as a sissy.

Present Tense in Narratives

> Writers sometimes use the present tense (simple present or present continuous) to tell about past events because it helps the reader feel closer to the events. For example, in paragraphs 3 and 4 Feynman tells about being forced to ask Barbara out when he was thirteen years old:
>
> . . . the guy next to me <u>gets</u> all excited. (simple present)
> He <u>pushes</u> her back, all the while saying in a loud voice . . . (simple present)
> Pretty soon the guys <u>are</u> all <u>standing</u> around me. . . . (present continuous)

Complete the items below.

1. Find other examples of this use of the simple present or present continuous tense in Feynman's writing in the paragraphs listed below.

   ¶6 _____

   ¶9 _____

   ¶11 _____

   ¶13 _____

   ¶14 _____

2. What events does Feynman describe using the narrative present?

   _____

RESPONDING TO READING

Discuss these questions.

1. This selection doesn't have a title. What title would you give it? Why?

2. A survey of American high school students done by *Choices* magazine (Feb./Mar. 2005) found that

   a. 72 percent of the students believe it's okay for girls to ask boys out.
   b. 63 percent would date someone who they think is physically unattractive.
   c. 56 percent would date someone their parents didn't like.
   d. 23 percent believe that honesty is the strongest quality of a successful romance.

   What do these findings tell you about dating in the United States nowadays? What do you think about girls asking boys out, dating someone who is not attractive, and dating someone your parents don't like? Do you think that honesty is the most important quality for a successful romance?

3. What are some dating customs in your country? If dating is not a custom in your country, how are marriage partners chosen?

CHAPTER 15

ABOUT THE READING

"Googling Your Date" is a feature article written for and distributed by the Associated Press (AP). AP is a cooperative news agency that shares ready-to-use news and feature articles with its members. Articles then appear in various newspapers at about the same time, sometimes with slightly different titles and subheads. This version appeared in *The Buffalo News* in April 2007.

BEFORE YOU READ

Thinking about the Topic

Discuss these questions.

1. What types of things do you want to know about people you might go out with?
2. What are some ways of learning these things?
3. How do people use the Internet, Google,® and social networking pages like Facebook to find out about other people?

Previewing

Read the title and subhead, and answer these questions.

1. What do you predict this article will be about?
2. What do you think "the dating dynamic" means?

Before you read, turn to Comprehension Check, First Reading, on page 97. Your purpose for the first reading is to be able to answer those questions.

READ

Googling Your Date

Love in the Age of the Internet: Online searches change the dating dynamic *By Martha Irvine*

fill in some of the blanks
a. give more information
b. take a test

1　　Dating used to be largely a matter of spending time with a love interest, discovering the good, the bad and the ugly in person. If you were lucky, friends helped **fill in some of the blanks**.

2　　These days, the Internet—and the ability to check people out before they ever meet up—has forever changed the rules.

3　　For better or worse, "googling" your date has become standard practice.

4　　"I often tell my friends that are still in the dating sphere to use the power of Google to their advantage," says Katie Laird, a 24-year-old Web marketing professional and self-proclaimed "social software geek"[1] from Houston.

(continued)

[1]**geek** *a computer expert*

enlightening
a. light
b. informative

turned up
a. found
b. made louder

initial
a. first
b. last

contend with
a. count on
b. deal with

5   The results can be **enlightening**, surprising—and sometimes, a little disturbing. So Laird's advice also comes with a warning: "Don't google what you can't handle."

6   Hers is the voice of experience. In her dating life, she regularly did online research on her dates and **turned up**, among other things, "bizarre" fetishes[2] and a guy who was fascinated with vampires.[3]

7   "Not my scene at all," Laird says, "and nothing I would've ever guessed over an **initial** meeting and beer."

8   She also had to **contend with** an on-again, off-again boyfriend who googled her on a daily basis to try and track her every move. The story did end happily, however, when she met her future husband online.

9   In some ways, having a social networking page—or pages—has become the new calling card.[4] It's a way for people to check out photos and find out what they have in common, even when they've already met in person.

10   That was the case for Brad White, a 23-year-old recent college grad[5] in Chicago, who met his current girlfriend through friends—and immediately looked her up on Facebook.

11   "The commonality of our music taste and friends is what prompted me to ask her out," White says, "obviously, besides the attraction."

12   The details people find also can provide a few talking points to get past the initial awkwardness of a first date—though not everyone likes to admit that they've done their research.

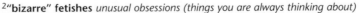

STAHLER.
SO TELL ME SOMETHING ABOUT YOURSELF THAT I HAVEN'T ALREADY GOOGLED.

www.comics.com   1/17   © 2008 by NEA, Inc.

13   "It seems like in contemporary dating, it's this elaborate dance between two people who already know a lot of what their date is talking about, but they can't admit it," says David Silver, an assistant professor of media studies at the University of San Francisco who studies online culture.

14   "You nod your head with curiosity, but you already know what they're going to say."

amazed at
a. very surprised by
b. very comfortable with

savvy
a. fear
b. knowledge

15   Even he is **amazed at** the level of information that can be dug up these days.

16   With a little creativity and Internet **savvy**, a person can find anything from blog postings[6] to news stories that might include personal details—and whether people are telling the truth about their age and where they've lived.

17   Dr. Paul Dobransky, a Chicago-based psychiatrist and author of *The Secret Psychology of How We Fall in Love,* says there's nothing wrong with doing a little online homework—but thinks the focus should remain on face-to-face interaction to make a final judgment.

18   "Our minds are more made for in-person, slow contact in getting to know one another," Dobransky says.

---

[2]**"bizarre" fetishes** *unusual obsessions (things you are always thinking about)*
[3]**vampires** *mythical creatures that bite people in the neck and suck their blood (e.g., Dracula)*
[4]**calling card** *a small card a with your name and address that people used to leave when they visited people*
[5]**grad** *short for* graduate
[6]**blog postings** *a blog is a Web log; a posting is something written and put on a blog (see glossary, Unit 3)*

issues
a. problems
b. solutions

19   Danielle Martinetti says online research really only helps to a point, anyway. "The crazy stuff usually becomes apparent on the actual date," the 30-year-old New Yorker says.

20   "No amount of online searching is going to tell you that a person has **issues** with his mother, loves to be described as a George Clooney[7] look-alike, has an overzealous obsession with hand sanitizer, or that he prefers to sit facing the door in a restaurant 'just in case.'"

---

[7]**George Clooney** an American movie actor

COMPREHENSION CHECK

First Reading

Answer these questions.

1. What Internet tools do people use to find out about someone they are dating or might date?
2. What is one way this changes face-to-face contact on a date?

Second Reading

A. Read the selection again. Mark the statements *T* (true) or *F* (false). Write the paragraph number(s) where you found evidence for each answer.

1. T F   In the past most of the information you got about people you dated came from friends.   ¶ ____

2. T F   Katie Laird advises her single friends to google their dates.   ¶ ____

3. T F   Katie Laird met her husband through the Internet.   ¶ ____

4. T F   Brad White googled his current girlfriend before he met her.   ¶ ____

5. T F   David Silver, who studies online culture, says it's amazing how much you can learn about a person on the Internet.   ¶ ____

6. T F   Paul Dobransky agrees that googling dates is the best way to get to know them quickly.   ¶ ____

7. T F   Danielle Martinetti used the Internet to find out that a guy she was dating had psychological problems.   ¶ ____

B. Choose the answer that correctly completes the sentence.

The main idea of this article is that

a. you can learn almost everything about a person you are interested in from the Internet, which will help you decide if you want to continue the relationship or not.

b. online dating services are an excellent and safe way to meet people, and you will already know a lot about them before you meet.

c. it is common to google people you are dating, but don't expect to find out everything; getting to know someone still takes time and personal contact.

Vocabulary Building

Read the underlined word or expression in its context and match it with the correct meaning. Use a dictionary if necessary.

____ 1. The results can be . . . a little <u>disturbing</u>. (¶5)

____ 2. . . . turned up . . . a guy who was <u>fascinated with</u> vampires. (¶6)

____ 3. . . . boyfriend who googled her on a daily basis to try and <u>track</u> her every move. (¶8)

____ 4. The commonality . . . is what <u>prompted</u> me to ask her out. . . . (¶11)

____ 5. It seems like in <u>contemporary</u> dating . . . (¶13)

____ 6. . . . it's this <u>elaborate</u> dance between two people who already know a lot of what their date is talking about. . . . (¶13)

____ 7. You nod your head with <u>curiosity</u>, but you already know what they are going to say. (¶14)

____ 8. . . . the <u>focus</u> should remain on face-to-face interaction to make a final judgment. (¶17)

____ 9. . . . made for in-person, slow <u>contact</u> in getting to know one another . . . (¶18)

____ 10. . . . an overzealous <u>obsession</u> with hand sanitizer . . . (¶20)

a. present day, modern

b. upsetting, something that causes worry

c. interest in knowing something

d. extremely interested in

e. something you cannot stop thinking about

f. communication

g. caused, made someone do something

h. complicated

i. follow

j. center of attention, main attention

Vocabulary Review

Complete the following statements about the reading selection with the correct word or expression from the list below. Use each word or expression only once.

contact	curious	initial
contemporary	disturbing	turn up

1. The Internet has brought a new dynamic to _____ dating. You can google anyone to find out about them, and you may be amazed by what you _____.

2. The things you learn about people are usually enlightening but sometimes _____.

3. Knowing something about a person before you meet him or her can help avoid the _____ awkwardness of a first date. But then you have to pretend you are _____ when you already know a lot about the person. That too can be uncomfortable.

4. In spite of all the information you find on the Internet, people really get to know each other through slow, face-to-face _____.

TEXT ANALYSIS *Paragraph Topics*

Reread or skim the selection. Match each set of paragraphs with the correct topic.

___ ¶1–3

___ ¶4–8

___ ¶9–11

___ ¶12–16

___ ¶17–18

___ ¶19–20

a. Danielle Martinetti's observations about what you can and can't learn by googling your date

b. getting to know people we date—past and present

c. Katie Laird's advice and experience

d. how we really get to know people we date according to Dr. Dobransky

e. how googling your date affects what happens on dates

f. the purpose of a social networking page with the example of Brad White

RESPONDING TO READING

Discuss these questions.

1. What could Katie Laird mean when she says in paragraph 5, "Don't google what you can't handle"?

2. Do you have a Facebook or MySpace page? Why or why not? What information about yourself do you put on your page if you have one?

3. How much of what you read on someone's social networking page do you believe?

CHAPTER 16

ABOUT THE READING

"Finding a Wife" is from *Small Faces,* a published collection of autobiographical essays. Gary Soto (1952–), an author and poet, grew up in Fresno, California. He has taught English and Chicano Studies at the University of California.

BEFORE YOU READ

Thinking about the Topic

Discuss these questions.

1. How did people you know meet their partners?
2. What, if anything, do you know about how married couples in other cultures meet?

Previewing

Read the title and the first three paragraphs. Choose the answer that correctly completes the sentence.

1. The narrator, the person who is telling the story, is a

   a. literature professor.   b. marriage counselor.   c. student.

2. He keeps thinking about the statement "It's easy to find a wife" because

   a. he doesn't want to forget it.

   b. he thinks he said something really smart.

   c. what he said may sound strange, but perhaps it's true.

3. Beginning with paragraph 3, the story

   a. continues in the same time frame.

   b. shifts to the future.

   c. shifts to the past.

Before you read, turn to Comprehension Check, First Reading, on page 103. Your purpose for the first reading is to be able to answer those questions.

You will also find questions to answer while you are reading. They will help you check your understanding and make predictions.

READ

chuckled
a. laughed
b. cried

wired
a. electrified, shocked
b. stimulated by coffee

Finding a Wife *By Gary Soto*

1   It's easy to find a wife, I told my students. Pick anybody, I said, and they **chuckled** and fidgeted in their chairs. I laughed a delayed laugh, feeling hearty and foolish as a pup[1] among these young men who were in my house to talk poetry and books. We talked, occasionally making sense, and drank cup after cup of coffee until we were so **wired** we had to stand up and walk around the block to shake out our nerves.

---

[1]**pup** *a puppy; a playful young dog*

argue
a. agree
b. disagree

ploy
a. order
b. trick

2   When they left I tried to write a letter, grade papers, and finally nap on the couch. My mind kept turning to how simple it is to find a wife, that we can easily say after a brief two- or three-week courtship, "I want to marry you."

3   When I was twenty, in college and living on a street that was a row of broken apartment buildings, my brother and I returned to our apartment from a game of racquetball to sit in the living room and **argue** whether we should buy a quart of beer. We were college poor, living off the cheap blessings of rice, raisins, and eggs that I took from our mom's refrigerator when Rick called her into the backyard about a missing sock from his laundry—a **ploy** from the start.

4   "Rick, I only got a dollar," I told him. He slapped his thigh and told me to wake up. It was almost the end of the month. And he was right. In two days our paychecks from Zak's Car Wash would burn like good report cards in our pockets[2]. So I gave in. I took the fifteen cents—a dime and five pennies—he had plucked from the ashtray of loose change in his bedroom, and went downstairs, across the street and the two blocks to Scott's Liquor. While I was returning home, swinging the quart of beer like a lantern[3], I saw the Japanese woman who was my neighbor, cracking walnuts on her front porch[4]. I walked slowly so that she looked up, smiling. I smiled, said hello, and continued walking to the rhythm of her hammer rising and falling.

5   In the apartment I opened the beer and raised it like a chalice[5] before we measured it in glasses, each of us suspicious that the other would get more. I rattled sunflower seeds onto a plate, and we pinched fingersful, the beer in our hands cutting loose a curtain of bubbles. We were at a party with no music, no host, no girls. Our cat, Mensa, dawdled in, blinking from the dull smoke of a sleepy afternoon. She looked at us, and we looked at her. Rick flicked a seed at her and said, "That's what we need—a woman!"

6   I didn't say anything. I closed my eyes, legs shot out in a V from the couch, and thought of that girl on the porch, the rise and fall of her hammer, and the walnuts cracking open like hearts.

What do you think the narrator will do next?

7   I got up and **peeked** from our two-story window that looked out onto a lawn and her apartment. No one. A wicker chair, potted plants, and a pile of

peeked
a. jumped
b. looked quickly

[2]**would burn like good report cards in our pockets** *children would hurry to take a good report card— a record of school grades sent home for parents—out of their pockets to show to their parents*

[3]**lantern**

[4]**porch**

[5]**chalice**

short of
a. before
b. inside

old newspapers. I looked until she came out with a broom to clean up the shells. "Ah, my little witch," I thought, and raced my heart downstairs, but stopped **short of** her house because I didn't know what to say or do. I stayed behind the hedge[6] that separated our yards and listened to her broom swish across the porch, then start up the walk to the curb.[7] It was then that I started to walk casually from behind the hedge and, when she looked at me with a quick grin, I said a hearty hello and walked past her without stopping to talk. I made my way to the end of the block where I stood behind another hedge, feeling foolish. I should have said something. "Do you like walnuts," I could have said, or maybe, "Nice day to sweep, isn't it?"—anything that would have my mouth going.

8   I waited behind that hedge, troubled by my indecision. I started back up the street and found her bending over a potted geranium, a jar of cloudy water in her hand. Lucky guy, I thought, to be fed by her.

9   I smiled as I passed, and she smiled back. I returned to the apartment and my bedroom, where I stared at my homework and occasionally looked out the window to see if she was busy on the porch. But she wasn't there. Only the wicker chair, the plants, the pile of newspapers.

How is the narrator behaving? What does it tell the reader? What do you think will happen next?

10   The days passed, white as clouds. I passed her house so often that we began to talk, sit together on the porch, and eventually snack on sandwiches that were thick as Bibles, with tumblers of milk to wash down her baked sweet bread flecked with tiny crushed walnuts.

screamed
a. shouted
b. wrote

11   After the first time I ate at her house, I hurried to the apartment to brag about my lunch to my brother, who was in the kitchen sprinkling raisins on his rice. Sandwiches, I **screamed**, milk, cold cuts,[8] chocolate ice cream! I spoke about her cupboards, creaking like ships weighed down with a cargo of rich food, and about her, that woman who came up to my shoulder. I was in love and didn't know where to go from there.

12   As the weeks passed, still white as clouds, we saw more of each other. Then it happened. On another Saturday, after browsing at a thrift shop[9] among gooseneck lamps and couches as jolly as fat men, we went to the west side of Fresno for Mexican food—menudo[10] for me and burritos[11] for her, with two beers clunked down on our table. When we finished eating and were ready to go, I wiped my mouth and plucked my **sole** five-dollar bill from my wallet as I walked to the cashier. It was all the big money I had. I paid and left the restaurant as if it were nothing, as if I spent such money every day. But inside I was thinking, "What am I going to do?"

sole
a. old
b. only

Is he acting cool? Why?

13   Scared as I was, I took Carolyn's hand into mine as we walked to the car. I **released** it to open the door for her. We drove and drove, past thrift shops she longed to browse through, but I didn't want to stop because I was scared

released
a. stopped holding
b. found

---

[6]**hedge** *See drawing of **porch** on page 101.*
[7]**curb** *See drawing of **curb** on page 101.*
[8]**cold cuts** *thin slices of cold, cooked meat*
[9]**thrift shop** *a store that sells used things at low prices*
[10]**menudo** *a popular dish among Mexican Americans that is made of beef stomach*
[11]**burritos** *beans and/or meat wrapped in a tortilla*

I would want to hold her hand again. After turning corners aimlessly, I drove back to her house where we sat together on the front porch, not touching. I was shivering, almost noticeably. But after a while, I did take her hand into mine and that space between us closed. We held hands, little tents opening and closing, and soon I nuzzled my face into her neck to find a place to kiss.

14   I married this one Carolyn Oda, a woman I found cracking walnuts on an afternoon. It was a chance meeting: I was walking past when she looked up to smile. It could have been somebody else, a girl drying persimmons on a line, or one hosing down her car, and I might have married another and been unhappy. But it was Carolyn, daughter of hard workers, whom I found cracking walnuts. She stirred them into dough that she shaped into loaves, baked in the oven, and set before me so that my mouth would keep talking in its search of the words to make me stay.

COMPREHENSION CHECK

First Reading

Answer these questions.

1. How did the narrator meet his wife?
2. Was it easy, as he said in the first sentence of the story, or did they have problems along the way?

Second Reading

Reread the parts of the story that will help you answer these questions.

1. What details show that the narrator and his brother didn't have much money when they were in college?

2. The narrator did things that showed he was interested in Carolyn. For example, he walked past her house slowly so she might notice him. What other details showed he was interested in her?

3. What, if anything, did Carolyn do to help the relationship develop?

4. What happened on their first date?

Vocabulary Building

Read the underlined word or expression in its context and match it with the correct meaning. Use a dictionary if necessary.

PART **1**

____ 1. . . . and <u>fidgeted</u> in their chairs. (¶1)

____ 2. I laughed . . . feeling hearty and <u>foolish</u>. . . . (¶1)

____ 3. . . . we can easily say after a brief two- or three-week <u>courtship</u>, "I want to marry you." (¶2)

____ 4. So I <u>gave in</u>. (¶4)

____ 5. . . . each of us <u>suspicious</u> that the other would get more. (¶5)

____ 6. . . . she looked at me with a quick <u>grin</u>. . . . (¶7)

a. a wide smile

b. finally agreed

c. afraid; not trusting the other

d. period of dating before marriage

e. moved a little because they were nervous or bored

f. stupid, silly

PART **2**

____ 7. . . . I <u>stared</u> at my homework. . . . (¶9)

____ 8. I hurried to the apartment to <u>brag</u> about my lunch to my brother. . . . (¶11)

____ 9. <u>Scared</u> as I was, I took Carolyn's hand. . . . (¶13)

____10. We drove . . . past thrift shops she <u>longed to</u> browse through. . . . (¶13)

____11. I was <u>shivering</u>, almost noticeably. (¶13)

____12. It was a <u>chance</u> meeting. . . . (¶14)

g. wanted to, had a strong desire to

h. tell in a proud way

i. unplanned, accidental

j. trembling (because of cold or nervousness)

k. looked at for a long time without moving the eyes

l. afraid, frightened

Handling Non-essential Vocabulary

Read each sentence and skip over the crossed-out words. Demonstrate that the word or words are not essential by answering the questions. If you are curious about the words, look them up in your dictionary.

1. I laughed a ~~delayed~~ laugh, feeling ~~hearty~~ and foolish as a pup. . . . (¶1)

   What did the narrator do? _____

   How did he feel? _____

2. We were college poor, living off the ~~cheap blessings~~ of rice, raisins, and eggs that I took from our mom's refrigerator. . . . (¶3)

   Did the narrator and his brother have much money? _____

   What did they eat? _____

3. I took the fifteen cents—a dime and five pennies—he had ~~plucked~~ from the ashtray ~~of loose change~~ in his bedroom. . . . (¶4)

What did he take? _____

Where was it? _____

4. I ~~rattled~~ sunflower seeds onto a plate, and we ~~pinched fingersful,~~ the beer in our hands ~~cutting loose a curtain of bubbles~~. (¶5)

What were the men eating with their beer? _____

Were they eating them from a bag, a jar, or a plate? _____

5. Our cat, Mensa, ~~dawdled~~ in, ~~blinking~~ from the ~~dull~~ smoke of a sleepy afternoon. (¶5)

Who entered the room? _____

6. Rick ~~flicked a seed~~ at her and said, "That's what we need—a woman!" (¶5)

What did the cat remind Rick that they needed? _____

7. A ~~wicker~~ chair, ~~potted~~ plants, and a ~~pile~~ of old newspapers. (¶7)

What was on the neighbor's porch? _____

8. . . . we began to talk, sit together on the porch, and eventually snack on sandwiches . . . with ~~tumblers~~ of milk ~~to wash down~~ her baked sweet bread ~~flecked~~ with ~~tiny crushed~~ walnuts. (¶10)

What did Carolyn and the narrator eat and drink? _____

What was in the bread? _____

9. On another Saturday, after ~~browsing~~ at a thrift shop among ~~gooseneck~~ lamps and couches . . . (¶12)

Where did Carolyn and the narrator go? _____

What are two things sold there? _____

10. . . . we went to the west side of Fresno for Mexican food—menudo for me and burritos for her, with two beers ~~clunked down~~ on our table. (¶12)

Where were the beers? _____

11. . . . and soon I ~~nuzzled~~ my face into her neck to find a place to kiss. (¶13)

Where did the narrator kiss Carolyn? _____

Vocabulary Review

Complete the following statements about the reading selection with the correct word or expression from the list below. Use each word or expression only once.

bragged	courtship	longed	short of
chance	foolish	scared	stared

1. This story is about how the narrator met his wife. He first saw her on her porch as he passed her house. Back in his apartment, he thought about her and peeked out the window because he _____ to see her again.

2. When she appeared with a broom, he ran downstairs but stopped _____ her house and hid behind a hedge. He was nervous and felt _____ because he didn't know what to say.

3. Later, at home, he _____ at his homework but couldn't concentrate.

4. Little by little they started talking. She invited him to have snacks and then lunch. He _____ about her good food to his brother.

5. He finally asked her out to eat at a Mexican restaurant. Sitting on her porch afterwards, he was _____ but finally kissed her.

6. His _____ of Carolyn was brief. It's surprising how such an important thing, like finding a wife, can develop from a _____ meeting.

TEXT ANALYSIS   *Story Development*

> Stories usually begin with a description of the characters and setting, or place. This stage is called the exposition. The next stage presents the rising action of the story, which leads to the high point, or climax. The climax is followed by the falling action, which then leads to the resolution, or *denouement.*

Write the letter of the correct description for each group of paragraphs in the Story Development diagram below.

a. the first real date
b. description of life as poor college students, seeing Carolyn for the first time
c. reflection/looking back
d. thinking about Carolyn and how to approach her
e. getting to know Carolyn better
f. the incident with students in the narrator's home that reminded him about how he met his wife

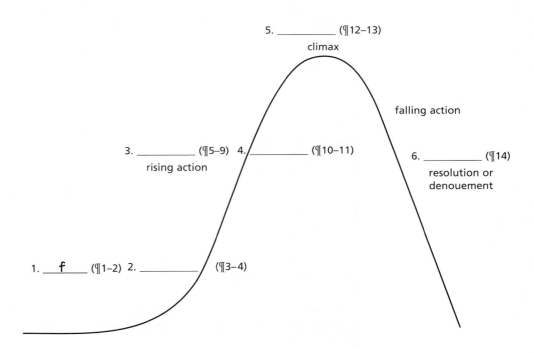

Story Development

RESPONDING TO READING

Discuss these questions.

1. Do you have any stories of how casual or chance meetings develop into something serious? Share them with your classmates.

2. How long do you think people should know each other before they decide to get married?

3. The couple in this story is an intercultural couple: Chicano and Japanese. What special problems, if any, might an intercultural couple have?

Extending Your Vocabulary

Word Families

Study the chart below to learn other forms of some of the words in this unit. If there is a box with a dash, either there is no word to fill it or the word is missing because it is not one you need to know now.

	NOUNS	VERBS	ADJECTIVES	ADVERBS
1.	amazement	amaze	amazing amazed	amazingly
2.	curiosity	—	curious	curiously
3.	embarrassment	embarrass	embarrassing embarrassed	—
4.	expectation	expect	expectant	expectantly
5.	fascination	fascinate	fascinated fascinating	—
6.	marriage	marry get married	married	—
7.	optimism	—	optimistic	optimistically
8.	satisfaction dissatisfaction	satisfy dissatisfy	satisfied, satisfactory dissatisfied, unsatisfactory	—
9.	sensitivity	sensitize	sensitive	sensitively
10.	suspicion	suspect	suspicious	suspiciously

For each item below, look at the row in the chart above with the same number. Choose the word that correctly completes the sentence. Be sure to use the correct form.

1. It's _____ how quickly Mara and Rama fell in love. Much
   to my _____, they are still together.

2. If you google someone, you must be _____ about them.

3. If you wear that red, orange, and purple dress, you will _____ me. I'll be _____ to be seen with you.

4. The course was OK, but it didn't meet my original _____. I thought it would be more interesting.

5. This guy's Facebook page is _____. I would really like to meet him.

6. If you _____ at a very young age, you may be sorry. What's the hurry?

7. She thought she would do well at her new job, so she started work with a great deal of _____.

8. Were you _____ with your grades last semester? Were your grades _____?

9. Cultural _____ is important when you travel or live in another country.

10. Why are you looking at me so _____? I haven't done anything.

Words with More Than One Meaning

Read each sentence. Match the underlined word or expression with the correct meaning. In some cases, you will use the same answer twice, and there may be more than one correct answer. An asterisk indicates a meaning that was used in this unit.

1. ___ Do you google a <u>date</u>* before you go out?

   ___ What's the <u>date</u> today?

   ___ Let's make a <u>date</u> for lunch one day next week.

a. a particular day of the month and year

b. a social appointment

c. someone you go out with (usually because you are in a romantic relationship)

2. ___ We normally get to know people through slow, face-to-face <u>contact</u>.*

   ___ If those wires make <u>contact</u>, you will get a shock.

   ___ I have a <u>contact</u> in the music industry; maybe she can help you.

   ___ Children come in <u>contact</u> with lots of germs in school.

a. state of touching or being close to

b. someone you know who may be able to help or advise you

c. communication

(continued)

3. ___ He has <u>issues</u>* with his mother.

   ___ You can find back <u>issues</u> of the magazine online.

   ___ At the next meeting, there are several <u>issues</u> to discuss.

   a. magazines or newspapers printed for a particular day, week, month, or year

   b. problems

   c. topics

4. ___ The students believe that their relationships will <u>keep</u>* getting better.

   ___ You can <u>keep</u> the book. I don't need it.

   ___ Some people <u>keep</u> all their e-mails.

   ___ The bread will <u>keep</u> longer if you put it in the refrigerator.

   a. not give back

   b. continue

   c. stay fresh, not spoil

   d. save, do not throw away

5. ___ All the students in the study were <u>single</u>.*

   ___ The <u>single</u> biggest problem many couples have is money.

   ___ I'll need a <u>single</u> for the copy machine.

   ___ It's harder to read <u>single</u>-spaced text than double-spaced text.

   a. one

   b. unmarried

   c. with only one space between lines

   d. one dollar bill

6. ___ Feynman's older friends <u>took</u> girls <u>out</u>.*

   ___ The dentist <u>took out</u> my wisdom teeth.

   ___ I have to <u>take</u> money <u>out</u> of the bank.

   a. removed

   b. went out on dates

WRITING

Choose one of the suggestions for writing below. Talk about what you plan to write with a classmate who chose the same topic. Then follow the instructions for writing.

1. Write a paragraph about choosing a partner. Check (✔) how important each item in the chart is to you. Then in a small group, discuss what you consider important in a partner.

Partner . . .	Very Important	Important	Not Very Important	Not Important at All
is good-looking				
is rich				
is hardworking				
is sociable				
is intelligent				
has same ethnic or religious background				
has similar political beliefs				
has a sense of humor				
(other)				

Based on the way you responded to the chart, write a paragraph about two or three things you think are important in choosing a partner. Start with a sentence like the one below and use words like *first, second,* and *finally* to help the reader follow your thoughts:

There are at least three things that I want in a romantic partner. First, . . .

2. Write a paragraph about how your parents met or how you met your partner, if you have one. Ask yourself *wh-* questions (*who, what, when, where, why, how*) to plan what you are going to say.

Try to use some of the following vocabulary in writing about the topic you choose: *advice, argue, ask out (go out with, take out), average, awkward, bother, can't stand, casual, chance, contact, contrary to, curiosity, cute, embarrassed/embarrassing, expect, fascinated, find out, foolish, initial, issues, lead to, nervous, optimistic, quit, scared, sensitive, single, sophisticated, stare, supposed to, suspicious, terrific, unrealistic.*

The Enterprising Spirit

Discuss

1. What does it take to be an entrepreneur—that is, to start a successful business?
2. Who can start a small business?
3. What is the importance of entrepreneurship to society and to individuals?

> Business . . . touches most lives at work, store, or home. It consumes growing proportions of our time, energies, ambitions, and emotions. Its ideas and language, of markets and motivation, have become dominant in politics and social life. We are all, to some degree, in business now, eagerly or reluctantly.
>
> Preface to *The Poetry of Business Life*, Ralph Windle, ed.

CHAPTER 17

ABOUT THE READING

"Entrepreneurs Recognize Opportunities" is an excerpt from a college textbook, *Entrepreneurship—Starting and Operating a Small Business* (2007) by Steve Mariotti.

BEFORE YOU READ

Thinking about the Topic

Discuss these questions.

1. Talk about what, if anything, you did as a youngster to make money.
2. What do you think of the idea of going into business for yourself? What are the risks? What are the benefits?
3. What would you do in the planning stages of starting a business?

Previewing

STUDY SKILL: READING TEXTBOOKS

- Read the Performance Objectives on page 114, which tell you what you should learn from reading the material.
- Read the headings.
- Notice boldfaced words; these are usually defined in the text, but often there is a glossary at the end of the book as well.
- Use the glossary of business terms on pages 140–141 as needed throughout the unit.
- Read in smaller chunks. This reading has been divided into three parts for you to do one part at a time.

Follow the suggestions in the box above, and then answer the questions.

1. What does the author want you to learn?
2. How is the material organized to help you learn?

Before you read each part, turn to Comprehension Check, First Reading, on page 118. Your purpose for reading each part is to be able to answer the questions for that part.

Entrepreneurs Recognize Opportunities *By Steve Mariotti*

Performance Objectives

- Explain what entrepeneurs do.
- Describe how free-enterprise economies work and how entrepeneurs fit into them.
- Explain how profit works as a signal to the entrepeneur.

PART 1: WHAT IS AN ENTREPRENEUR?[1]

1   Have you ever eaten a Mrs. Fields® cookie? Used an Apple® computer? Listened to a hip-hop CD? An entrepreneur brought each of these products into your world.

2   Debbi Fields was a young mother with no business experience when she started selling her chocolate chip cookies. Today, Mrs. Fields Cookies has over 650 stores in the United States, and over 65 locations in 11 other countries. Steve Jobs and Stephen Wozniak were **barely** out of college when they invented the personal computer in a garage in Cupertino, California. Now Apple sells millions of iBooks, iPods, and other innovative products each year. Russell Simmons used his own passion for hip-hop to turn rap artists like Run DMC and LL Kool J into international pop stars. Simmons and his businesses—Def Jam Records, Rush Communications, etc.—have come to be worth over $300 million.

3   Most Americans earn money by working in business. **Business** is the buying and selling of products or services in order to make money.

- A **product** is something that exists in nature or is made by human beings. It is *tangible,* meaning that it can be touched.
- A **service** is work that provides time, skills, or **expertise** in exchange for money. It is *intangible.* You cannot actually touch it.

Someone who earns a living by working for someone else's business is an **employee** of that business. There are many kinds of employees. At Ford Motor Company, for instance, some employees build the cars, some sell the cars, and some manage the company. But employees all have one thing in common—they do not own a business; they work for others who do. They know how much money they can earn, and that amount is limited to salary, plus bonuses, and any stock options they may receive.

4   Some people start their own businesses and work for themselves. They are called **entrepreneurs**. Entrepreneurs are often both owners and employees. For an entrepreneur, the sky is the limit as far as earnings are concerned. Unlike an employee, an entrepreneur owns the profit that his or her business earns and may choose whether to reinvest it in the business or use it to pay him- or herself.

---

[1] *The ideas and concepts in this chapter are adapted from the works of Jeffry A. Timmons, Howard W. Stevenson, and William Bygrave.*

barely
a. illegally
b. just recently

expertise
a. knowledge
b. money

surfaced
a. appeared
b. looked

shifts
a. moves
b. destroys

5   An entrepreneur is someone who recognizes an opportunity to start a business that other people may not have noticed—and jumps on it. As economist Jeffry Timmons writes in the preface of *New Venture Creation: Entrepreneurship for the 21st Century,* "A skillful entrepreneur can shape and create an opportunity where others see little or nothing—or see it too early or too late."

6   The word *entrepreneur* first **surfaced** in France in the seventeenth century. It was used to describe someone who undertook a project, but after awhile it came to mean someone who starts a new business—often a new kind of business or a new (and improved) way of doing business. The French economist Jean Baptiste Say wrote at the turn of the nineteenth century: "The entrepreneur **shifts** economic resources [like wood or coal] out of an area of lower and into an area of higher productivity and greater yield." By doing this, Say argued, entrepreneurs add value to **scarce resources**. Oil is a resource because it is used as fuel. Wood is a resource because it can be used to make a house or a table or paper. Economists consider all resources that cost money "scarce."

7   Debbi Fields took resources—eggs, butter, flour, sugar, and chocolate chips—and turned them into cookies. People liked what she did with those resources so much that they were willing to pay her more for the cookies than it cost her to buy the resources to make them. She added value to the resources she purchased by what she did with them—and created a multimillion dollar business in the process.

PART 2: THE ECONOMIC QUESTIONS[2]

8   Since time began, people have had to answer the same basic questions:

- What should be produced?
- When will it be produced?
- How will it be produced?
- Who will produce it?
- Who gets to have what is produced?

Families and individuals, as well as businesspeople, charities, corporations, and governments, all have had to answer these questions. The system a group of people creates through making these decisions is called an **economy**. The study of how these different groups answer these questions is called **economics**.

9   An economy is a country's financial structure. It is the system that produces and distributes wealth in a country. The U.S. economy is called a **free-enterprise system** because anyone is free to start a business. You do not have to get permission from the government to start a business, although you do have to obey laws and regulations.

10   This economic system is also called **capitalism** because the money used to start a business is called **capital**. Anyone who can raise the capital is free to start a business. You can start a business!

Voluntary Exchange

11   The free-enterprise system is also sometimes referred to as a "free-trade system" because it is based on **voluntary exchange**. Voluntary exchange is a trade between two **parties** who agree to trade money for a product or service. No one is forced to trade. Each is excited by the opportunity the trade offers. Both parties agree to the exchange because they both benefit.

parties
a. social gatherings
b. people or groups

12   Let's say you have a contracting business and your busy neighbors hire you to renovate their kitchen. You need money and are willing to use your skills and time to earn it. They want their kitchen renovated and are willing to give up money to get it done. You each have something the other wants, so you are willing to trade. Trading only takes place when both parties believe they will benefit.

(continued)

---

[2]Source of definitions: *Small Business Administration*

Free Trade

For centuries, international trade was very difficult. To sell products in another country required long and dangerous journeys over land or by ship. Many countries were closed to outside trade. Governments also used their power to give their own businesspeople a competitive advantage over those from other countries by imposing trade barriers, such as taxes on foreign goods that made them too expensive to buy. Governments could also enforce restrictions on how many imports or exports could cross a country's borders.

Today, trade barriers are falling in most parts of the world. The North American Free Trade Agreement (NAFTA) of 1994 ended trade barriers between the United States, Mexico, and Canada. This turned the entire continent into a free-trade zone. The General Agreement on Tariffs and Trade (GATT) cut or **eliminated** tariffs between 117 countries. Where people are free to trade voluntarily to as large a market as possible, their ability to find someone to buy their goods or services increases. So does their ability to meet consumer needs.

Meanwhile, the Internet has made it much easier for entrepreneurs to sell to customers all over the world. Shipping, too, has become much faster and less expensive. It is an exciting time to be in business!

eliminated
a. created
b. removed

competition
a. more than one company trying to win customers
b. sports or games

Benefits of Free Enterprise

13   We all benefit from living in a free-enterprise system because it discourages entrepreneurs who waste resources—by driving them out of business. It encourages entrepreneurs who use resources efficiently to satisfy consumer needs—by rewarding them with profit.

14   We also benefit because free enterprise encourages **competition** between entrepreneurs. Someone who can make cookies that taste as good as Mrs. Fields Cookies, and sells them at a lower price, will eventually attract Mrs. Fields Cookies customers. This will force Mrs. Fields Cookies to lower prices to stay competitive. Consumers benefit because they get to buy cookies at a lower price.

What Is a "Small" Business?

15   The public often thinks of business only in terms of "big" business—companies such as General Electric®, Ford®, Microsoft®, McDonald's®, and Nike®. A big business is defined by the Small Business Administration as having more than one hundred employees and selling more than $5 million worth of products or services in a year.

16   Most of the world's businesses are small businesses. A neighborhood restaurant or a clothing boutique are examples of small businesses. A small business employs fewer than one hundred employees and has yearly sales under $5 million.

17   Surprisingly, the principles involved in running a large company like MTV and a corner deli are the same. In fact, most multimillion dollar businesses in this country started out as small, entrepreneurial ventures. This is why entrepreneurship is often called the "engine" of our economy. It "drives" the economy, creating wealth and jobs and improving our standard of living.

initially
a. finally
b. at first

eventually
a. after a long time
b. before starting

PART 3: A BUSINESS MUST MAKE A PROFIT TO STAY IN BUSINESS

18   No matter how big or small, a business must make a **profit**; that is, the amount of money coming in must be greater than the amount of money required to pay the bills. Most businesses do lose money **initially** because they have to lay out cash to set up operations and advertise to attract customers. If the business cannot make a profit, **eventually** the entrepreneur will be unable to pay the bills and will have to close.

19   Closing a business is nothing to be ashamed of if you learn from the experience. In fact, most successful entrepreneurs open and close more than one business during their lives. If your venture is not making a profit after you have gotten it up and running, that is a signal that you may be in the wrong business. Closing it may be the smartest decision.

20   An entrepreneur may change businesses many times over a lifetime in response to changing competition and consumer needs. The great economist Joseph Schumpeter called the process of constantly changing businesses "creative destruction."[3]

Profit Is the Sign That the Entrepreneur Is Adding Value

21   Profit is the sign that an entrepreneur has added value to the scarce resources he or she is using. Debbi Fields added value to scarce resources by creating something with them that people were willing to buy for a price that gave her a profit. In contrast, not making a profit is a sign that the entrepreneur is not using resources very well and is not adding value to them.

The Desire to Make Money Is Not a Good Reason to Start a Business

22   Starting a business is an opportunity, and like any opportunity it should be evaluated by taking a close look at the costs and benefits it offers. One thing is for certain, though, *the desire to make money alone, is not a good enough reason to start one's own business.*

23   The financial rewards of owning your own business may not happen until you put in years of hard work. The desire to make money may not be enough to keep you going through the difficult early period. Most successful companies have been founded by an entrepreneur with a powerful and motivating dream.

---

[3]*Joseph A. Schumpeter,* Capitalism, Socialism, and Democracy *(New York: Harper & Row, 1942).*

COMPREHENSION CHECK

First Reading

Answer these questions.

PART 1

1. What is an entrepreneur?
2. What is an employee?
3. What is the difference?

PART 2

1. What is a free-enterprise economy?
2. What are its benefits?

PART 3

1. Why is profit important?
2. Why should profit *not* be an entrepreneur's major motivation?

Second Reading

Read each part again, as well as the box entitled Global Impact—Free Trade. Highlight or take notes to answer the questions.

PART 1

1. What are some examples of adding value to a resource?
2. How do most Americans earn their living?
3. What's the difference between a product and a service?
4. What is the origin of the word *entrepreneur*?
5. How do entrepreneurs see problems?
6. How is the word *scarce* in the business term *scarce resources* used differently from its ordinary use?

PART 2

1. Why is capitalism called capitalism?
2. What is the difference between a small and a large business? Which is more common?
3. What is the role of competition in the free-enterprise system? How does competition benefit the consumer?
4. Why is entrepreneurship called the "engine" of an economy?

PART 3

1. What is profit, and what does it indicate about a business?
2. How should entrepreneurs react if their business fails?

GLOBAL IMPACT—FREE TRADE

1. What is a tariff?
2. Why is international trade easier now than ever before?
3. Does the term *free trade* in paragraph 11 have exactly the same meaning as in the box?

Vocabulary Building

Read the underlined word or expression in its context and match it with the correct meaning. Use a dictionary if necessary.

PART 1

____ 1. Now Apple sells . . . other <u>innovative</u> products each year. (¶2)

____ 2. . . . an entrepreneur . . . may choose whether to <u>reinvest</u> it (profit) in the business. . . . (¶4)

____ 3. . . . someone who <u>undertook</u> (past tense of *undertake*) a project . . . (¶6)

____ 4. The entrepreneur shifts economic <u>resources</u> . . . into an area of higher productivity and greater yield. (¶6)

____ 5. . . . your busy neighbors hire you to <u>renovate</u> their kitchen. (¶12)

____ 6. It (free enterprise) encourages entrepreneurs who use resources efficiently . . . by <u>rewarding</u> them with profit. (¶13)

a. remodel, repair

b. something that can be used to increase wealth

c. put money back into a business

d. started to do work for which you are responsible

e. giving or paying

f. new, different, better

PART 2

____ 7. The <u>public</u> often thinks of business only in terms of "big" business. . . . (¶15)

____ 8. . . . most multimillion dollar businesses . . . started out as small, entrepreneurial <u>ventures</u>. (¶17)

____ 9. . . . any opportunity . . . should be <u>evaluated</u> by taking a close look at the costs and benefits it offers. (¶22)

____10. . . . an entrepreneur with a powerful and <u>motivating</u> dream. (¶23)

____11. Governments also used their power . . . by <u>imposing trade barriers</u>. . . . (Global Impact—Free Trade box)

____12. Governments could also <u>enforce restrictions</u> on how many imports or exports could cross a country's borders. (Global Impact—Free Trade box)

g. introducing means, such as taxes, in order to block or prevent trade

h. providing a strong reason to do something

i. business activities that involve risk

j. carefully considered and judged

k. make people obey rules that set limits

l. ordinary people

Vocabulary Review

Complete the following statements about the reading selection with the correct word or expression from the list below. Use each word or expression only once.

competition   innovative   resources
evaluate   regulations   venture
eventually

1. Not everyone is willing to undertake a business _____, but we all benefit from the products and services that entrepreneurs provide.

2. In a free-enterprise economy, anyone can start a business, but you need start-up capital, and you do have to obey laws and _____.

3. Entrepreneurs take _____ and add value to them, and consumers pay for the product or service.

4. It helps if entrepreneurs have a(n) _____ idea for starting a business, and it's important to _____ the idea before investing a lot of money.

5. One of the good things about capitalism is that it encourages _____—that is, a number of businesses providing the same goods or services—which forces producers to increase quality and to reduce prices.

6. Although it may take time, entrepreneurs have to make a profit _____. If they don't, they will have to change businesses, which is neither unusual nor necessarily bad.

Definitions Found in the Text

When you study a new field, a major part of the job is learning new concepts and specialized vocabulary. Textbooks often have glossaries, and good students, including native speakers, need to use them. Another place you find definitions is in the text itself. In this selection, terms defined in the text are printed in boldface, and some are in italics.

Locate the definitions for the following words in the reading selection (or the glossary) and make word bank cards for them. (See page xx of the Introductory Chapter.)

1. business
2. product
3. tangible
4. service
5. intangible
6. employee
7. entrepreneur
8. scarce resources
9. economy
10. economics
11. free-enterprise system
12. capitalism
13. capital
14. voluntary exchange
15. profit

RESPONDING TO READING

Discuss these questions.

1. What personal characteristics should an entrepreneur have?

2. What are the personal costs of starting and running your own business?

3. Is free trade always good? What are its advantages and disadvantages?

4. What are some ideas for an innovative small business you might like to start?

CHAPTER 18

ABOUT THE READING

"I, Lender" is an interview with a young *software engineer,* someone who writes computer programs. It appeared in a special issue of *Smithsonian* magazine, fall 2007, which presented thirty-seven young innovators in the arts and sciences. Matt Flannery and his wife became interested in microlending after learning about it through her job. *Microlending,* first implemented by Mohammad Yunus and the Grameen Bank in Bangladesh, is the lending of small amounts of money to poor entrepeneurs, primarily in developing countries. Flannery's business, Kiva.org, illustrates how microlending has become a successful way to lift people out of poverty.

BEFORE YOU READ

Thinking about the Topic

Discuss these questions.

1. What kind of websites have the extension *.org* in their Internet address?
2. What sites of this kind, if any, do you visit? Why do you visit them?
3. What types of entrepreneurs might benefit from microlending—that is, receiving a small loan?

Previewing

Read the title, by-line, and subhead. Read paragraph 1, scan the headings, and answer the questions.

1. Who are Matt Flannery and Amy Crawford?
2. What are the boldfaced headings?
3. What are the paragraphs under them?
4. What is the purpose of the Internet site, Kiva.org?

Before you read, turn to Comprehension Check, First Reading, on page 124. Your purpose for the first reading is to be able to answer those questions.

READ

I, Lender *Interviewed by Amy Crawford*

Software engineer Matt Flannery pioneers Internet microloans to the world's poor

1   MATT FLANNERY, 30, cofounded the nonprofit Kiva.org, a microlending site, in 2004. Kiva operates on a people-to-people model, allowing private individuals to make loans to borrowers seeking to **establish** small businesses in developing countries.

establish
a. start, set up
b. close down

How does Kiva work?

2   Kiva connects individual lenders from the developed world to individual borrowers in the developing world. We work with local microfinance institutions that post the loan applications they get on the Internet. Kiva raises debt capital via the Internet from thousands of lenders in the United States and Europe. The partner institutions sort and administer loans, but our lenders actually fund them.

How did you get this idea?

3   My wife [Jessica, cofounder of Kiva] was consulting in microfinance in East Africa, and I went along on a trip with her. We had the idea together. I thought it would be interesting to give people the chance to participate as partners, not just donors, with [small] businesses in Africa. I've always been interested in ideas about poverty. I've been sponsoring children[1] through my church my whole life. It was part of my upbringing. What we're doing now is an extension of that personal history.

Why loans rather than donations?

4   Lending to somebody sends the message that you're treating them as an equal, someone who can participate with you in a business relationship. It's a really dignified way to interact with people.

What challenges did you have to overcome as you were setting up Kiva?

5   We started Kiva without any funding, and whenever you do something like that, it's hard to prepare for growth. Without a lot of start-up capital, you have to bootstrap[2] your way at every step. At one point, we were getting thousands of users, and we had a $20 Web-hosting plan[3] on a shared server,[4] so our website was crashing.[5] We had to figure out in one weekend how to transfer the site from that commercial hosting plan.

How do you make sure the loans are not misused?

6   We're as transparent as possible. When you loan on the website, you get to choose whom you loan to—a goat-herding business, a retail business, a fruit stand. Most of the time, you hear back about what happened [through the website]. We allow the lenders to ask questions and the partners to report. This summer we sent about 30 volunteers—we call them Kiva fellows—to witness Kiva's impact firsthand, and they're writing about it on the website. Just about every minute, there's a new journal entry.

So far, Kiva has an excellent repayment record. How do you manage that?

7   Repayment rates in the microfinance industry are much higher than for U.S. domestic loans. That's because microfinance institutions are lending to people for whom getting a loan is their only shot at anything. If you're given a sixty-dollar loan, your chance of getting another loan **is contingent on** you paying that back.

You're also a lender on Kiva. Who are some of the people you've lent to personally?

8   I usually lend to Eastern Europeans—a food market in Azerbaijan, a clothing store in Ukraine. Most of my portfolio is people from Azerbaijan, Moldova, Tajikistan, Bulgaria, places like that, because they are the least popular borrowers on the site, and they often **get overlooked** by our lenders.

is contingent on
a. depends on
b. keeps on

get overlooked
a. are remembered
b. are not noticed

[1]**sponsoring children** *making regular donations to an organization that helps take care of poor children*
[2]**bootstrap** *to find creative ways to support a start-up business until it becomes profitable*
[3]**Web-hosting plan** *an arrangement where you pay a small fee for an agency to put your website on the Internet*
[4]**shared server** *a large computer connected to the Internet that is never switched off and provides Internet access for many different customers' websites*
[5]**crashing** *failing*

First Reading

Answer these questions.

1. How does Kiva raise capital for microlending?
2. Why does Kiva make loans rather than giving money away as donations?

Second Reading

Read the selection again. Mark the statements *T* (true) or *F* (false). Write the paragraph number(s) where you found evidence for each answer.

1. T F Kiva matches private lenders from richer countries to entrepreneurs in poorer countries.   ¶ ____

2. T F Kiva is a local microfinance institution in East Africa.   ¶ ____

3. T F The Flannerys' motivation for establishing Kiva was primarily to make a big profit.   ¶ ____

4. T F Starting Kiva required a lot of capital.   ¶ ____

5. T F Kiva attracted thousands of potential lenders.   ¶ ____

6. T F From the beginning Kiva owned the server that connected them to the Internet.   ¶ ____

7. T F Lenders at Kiva can choose what business to lend to.   ¶ ____

8. T F At Kiva, there is good communication between lenders and borrowers.   ¶ ____

9. T F The repayment rates are good for microloans because people want to be able to borrow again in the future.   ¶ ____

10. T F Flannery lends to people in Eastern Europe because other lenders tend to overlook that part of the world.   ¶ ____

Vocabulary Building

Read the underlined word or expression in its context and match it with the correct meaning. Use a dictionary if necessary.

____ 1. . . . Matt Flannery <u>pioneers</u> Internet microloans to the world's poor. (subhead)

____ 2. The partner institutions <u>sort</u> and administer loans. . . . (¶2)

____ 3. . . . but our lenders actually <u>fund</u> them. (¶2)

____ 4. . . . give people the chance to participate as partners, not just <u>donors,</u> with [small] businesses in Africa. (¶3)

____ 5. It was part of my <u>upbringing.</u> (¶3)

____ 6. It's a really <u>dignified</u> way to interact with people. (¶4)

____ 7. We're as <u>transparent</u> as possible. (¶6)

____ 8. . . . we sent about 30 volunteers . . . to <u>witness</u> Kiva's impact firsthand. . . . (¶6)

a. care and training that parents give their children

b. clear

c. is the first one to do something

d. provide the money for

e. people who give something

f. see

g. respectful, showing person's worth

h. arrange in groups, categorize

Using a Dictionary

Write the number of the meaning in the dictionary entry below that best defines the underlined word as it is used in the sentence. You may have to extend one of the meanings to a new situation. You may want to use the dictionary definition and example sentence when you add some of these words to your word bank.

1. . . . local microfinance institutions that <u>post</u> the loan applications they get on the Internet. (¶2)

   Definition # _____

> **post** poust *v.* [T] **1** to put a public notice about something on a wall or BULLETIN BOARD: *They've posted warning signs on the gate.* **2** to give someone a government job in a foreign country: *Officials posted in the area were told to leave.* **3** if a company posts its profits, sales, losses, etc., it records the money gained or lost in its accounts: *In the final quarter, the company posted $12.4 million in earnings.*

(continued)

2. Kiva <u>raises</u> debt capital via the Internet. . . . (¶2)   **Definition #** _____

> **raise** /reɪz/ v. [T]
>
> **1** ▶MOVE◀ to move or lift something to a higher position or to an upright position: *The flag is raised at school every morning.* | *Raise your hand if you know the answer.*
>
> **2** ▶INCREASE◀ to increase an amount, number, or level: *a plan to raise taxes* | *Don't raise your voice at me, young man.* (=speak loudly and angrily)
>
> **3** ▶IMPROVE◀ to improve the quality or standard of something: *This bill is all about raising standards in our schools.*
>
> **4** ▶CHILDREN/ANIMALS/CROPS◀ to take care of children, animals, or crops until they are fully grown: *They've raised seven children.* | *He wants to try raising corn.*
>
> **5** ▶GET MONEY/SUPPORT◀ to collect money, support, etc. so that you can use it to help people: *We've raised $10,000 for cancer research.*

3. How do you <u>manage</u> that? (¶7)   **Definition #** _____

> **man·age** /ˈmænɪdʒ/ v. [I,T] **1** to succeed in doing something difficult, such as dealing with a problem, living in a difficult situation: *It was heavy, but I managed to get it up the stairs.* | *I don't know how we'll manage* (=how we'll buy the things we need) *now that Keith's lost his job.* **2** to direct or control a business and the people who work in it : *I spent 16 years managing a hotel in Wilmington.* **3** SPOKEN HUMOROUS to do something that causes problems: *The kids managed to spill paint all over the carpet.*

4. . . . getting a loan is their only <u>shot</u> at anything. (¶7)   **Definition #** _____

> **shot** /ʃɑt/ n.
>
> **1** ▶GUNS◀ an act of firing a gun: *Troops fired a warning shot.*
>
> **2** ▶DRUG◀ the act of putting medicine or legal drugs into your body using a needle: *Have you had your flu shot?*
>
> **3** ▶MOVIES/PHOTOGRAPHS◀ **a)** a photograph: *a beautiful shot of the countryside around Prague* **b)** the view of something in a movie, television program, or photograph: *close-up shots of the actress*
>
> **4** ▶ATTEMPT◀ INFORMAL an attempt to do something or achieve something: *Marty always wanted to take a shot at acting.*

5. Most of my <u>portfolio</u> is people from Azerbaijan. . . . (¶8)   **Definition #** _____

> **port·fo·li·o** /pɔrtˈfouliˌou/ n. **1** a large, flat case used for carrying drawings, documents, etc. **2** a collection of drawings or other pieces of work by an artist, photographer, etc. **3** a collection of SHARES owned by a particular person or company: *an investment portfolio*

Vocabulary Review

Complete the following statements about the reading selection with the correct word or expression from the list below. Use each word or expression only once.

dignified	post	sort
microloans	raise	transparent
pioneered	shot	witness

1. Matt Flannery and his wife Jessica cofounded Kiva.org, an Internet site that helps entrepreneurs in the developing world _____ capital for their businesses.

2. The Flannerys believe in _____ rather than donations because loans are a _____ way of helping people.

3. This is the way it works: People in developing countries apply for loans to local microfinance institutions in their own countries. These institutions _____ the loans into categories and then _____ applications on the Internet, where lenders choose a business to lend to.

4. Everything at the Kiva site is very _____. Lenders and borrowers can communicate with each other. Kiva volunteers have traveled to developing countries to _____ the impact of Kiva on small businesses.

5. Repayment of microloans is very high because if borrowers don't pay back the loan, they won't have a _____ at getting any more help.

6. Muhammad Yunus and the Grameen Bank won the Nobel Peace Prize for the use of microcredit to lift people out of poverty, but the Flannerys _____ the idea on the Internet.

TEXT ANALYSIS   Interview Format

Answer these questions.

1. How does the way in which this reading is set on the page—the formatting—tell you it is an interview?
2. What about this format makes it easy to read?
3. If you didn't find this interview easy to read, what was difficult about it?

RESPONDING TO READING

Discuss these questions.

1. Why is microfinancing a good thing?

2. Matt Flannery had an innovative idea. How do people come up with innovative ideas? Do you think age has anything to do with it? Explain.

CHAPTER 19

ABOUT THE READING

"How to Be Fair" is from the June 15, 2005, issue of *American Way,* the magazine of American Airlines.

BEFORE YOU READ

Thinking about the Topic

Discuss these questions.

1. If you were a farmer or an artisan, how would you market or sell your products? What would you do to get the best price?
2. Who else makes money from your products before they get to the consumer?
3. What do you think the term *fair trade* means?

Previewing

Read the title and the subhead, and answer the questions.

1. What are some fair-trade products, and where can people buy them?
2. What does the question in the subhead tell us about the author's purpose?

Before you read, turn to Comprehension Check, First Reading, on page 130. Your purpose for the first reading is to be able to answer those questions.

READ

How to Be Fair *By Karen M. Kroll*

You've seen fair-trade coffee at the donut shop, fair-trade clothing online, fair-trade gifts in your favorite catalog. So how does trade get to be fair, anyway?

1   On most farms, tractors[1] are standard equipment. But the Poco Fundo Fair-Trade Cooperative in Brazil isn't like most farms. It's in the developing world, for one thing, where animal power is as common as horsepower.[2] Until last year, Poco Fundo's member farmers handled planting and harvesting the old-fashioned way—by hand.

mechanical help
a. animals
b. machines

2   Two words explain why the co-op[3] was finally able to afford **mechanical help:** *fair trade.* With earnings from selling coffee through a fair-trade network to buyers such as Dunkin' Brands—which operates Dunkin' Donuts®—co-op members bought their first tractor.

---

[1]**tractor**

[2]**horsepower** *used here to mean "machinery," normally a unit for measuring the power of an engine, for example, 75 hp*

[3]**co-op** *short for* cooperative; *a business owned equally by the workers*

concept
a. idea
b. error

table linens
a. bed sheets
b. tablecloths, napkins

wares
a. clothing
b. products

enable
a. make it possible for
b. make it difficult for

3   And that's just one example of how fair trade is changing the way business is done. Many workers who grow products certified as fair trade, labor on small farms or workshops in developing countries, and they earn enough to cover their costs, invest in their businesses, and have a small profit left over.

4   Before fair trade, the same workers earned much less for the same products, often only enough to survive. "The small farmer is often dealing with intermediaries who take a disproportionate share of the revenue," says Jim Cleaves, manager of the green coffee-supply chain with Dunkin' Brands. And it's that intermediary that fair trade aims to eliminate.

5   The **concept** of fair trade is far from new. In the 1940s, Edna Ruth Byler, a Mennonite volunteer, traveled to Puerto Rico, where she met a group of women who were embroidering[4] beautiful **table linens** but had no way to market them outside their own village.

6   So Byler brought a few pieces back to her hometown of Akron, Pennsylvania, and showed them to women's groups and to churches. She found a ready market— and launched what would become Ten Thousand Villages, now a 105-store retail chain that rang up some $15 million in sales last year.

7   Today, buyers for Ten Thousand Villages work directly with 110 artisan groups in 32 countries, from Bangladesh to Nepal to Vietnam. They traverse dirt roads in four wheel-drive vehicles to meet artisans at their homes and workshops. Then, the selected artisans package their **wares** for shipment and take them by truck to the nearest port, where they're loaded on a ship and transported to North America—a process that can take up to eight weeks.

8   World of Good, another fair-trade retail distributor, is borrowing from a business model used by greeting card companies. It sells fair-trade handicrafts through kiosks[5] in book, gift, and grocery stores. Since its launch in 2004, the company has inked deals with 60 stores in the San Francisco area, and it's now in discussions to supply fair-trade goods to a national department store chain, says cofounder Priya Haji.

9   So how, exactly, does fair trade work? Retailers of fair-trade products work as directly as possible with the farmers and artisans, to reduce the need for middlemen and allow more of the retail price to be passed on to the original producer. To compensate, the producers organize into cooperatives and take on responsibilities the middlemen otherwise would perform. For instance, a cooperative might purchase a truck for its farmers to transport their wares. Meanwhile, the buyers often help producers with product development; some even offer financing so their producers always have access to operating capital.

10   "The producers are paid prices that **enable** them to have reasonable resources for their farms and communities," says Kate McKone-Sweet, an associate professor of management at Babson College. "In return, buyers are able to obtain high-quality products and develop a sustainable supply chain."

11   To verify that the farmers and artisans get a fair-trade price—one that can provide a living wage and leave enough for producers to reinvest in their businesses—independent groups audit the books of both the fair-trade producers and the distributors who buy from them. At the auditor's okay, the distributors can label the products as certified fair-trade goods. TransFair USA is the certifying group in the United States, and similar groups work in 16 other developed countries.

(continued)

---

[4]**embroidering** *sewing a picture or pattern on cloth with colored thread*
[5]**kiosk** *small space for selling goods*

12   For farm products, the costs of growing crops are fairly simple to calculate, so coming up with an acceptable fair-trade price is pretty **straightforward.** When it comes to handicrafts, though, the amount of labor and materials—not to mention the skills required—to create different products varies wildly, says Siddharth Sanghvi, World of Good cofounder. Currently, no formal certification process for these items exists.

13   To come up with fair-trade prices for its goods, Ten Thousand Villages has its buyers interview suppliers about the amount of time and materials required for each particular product. In addition, they commit to purchasing from its artisans on an **ongoing,** consistent basis and to paying for goods in advance so that the workers don't have to wait to get paid. When deciding which products to sell, the company chooses crafts that reinforce cultural traditions and that are made using environmentally sensitive methods.

14   To be sure, working within the fair-trade supply chain presents challenges. Many farmers and artisans lack easy access to tools that U.S. businesses take for granted, such as computers and phones. Most live in developing countries without strong transportation systems. Political upsets are an ongoing risk.

15   Given the challenges, why bother with fair trade? Ten Thousand Villages enables the artisans it works with to support themselves and their families. TransFair USA reports that more than a million family farmers in developing countries have seen their incomes rise as a result of fair trade. The farmers who supply Dunkin' Brands with fair-trade espresso have earned an additional $3.1 million. Clearly, consumers who buy fair-trade items are doing more than just consuming.

COMPREHENSION CHECK

First Reading

Answer these questions.

1. How does fair trade work?
2. Who benefits the most? Why?

Second Reading

A. Read the selection again. Mark the statements *T* (true) or *F* (false). Write the paragraph number(s) where you found evidence for each answer.

1. T F   The Poco Fundo Fair-Trade Cooperative has had farm machinery for a long time.   ¶ ___

2. T F   Fair trade eliminates middlemen so that farmers and artisans get a larger profit.   ¶ ___

3. T F   Fair trade is a twenty-first century idea.   ¶ ___

4. T F   Ten Thousand Villages is an example of a small business that has become a large one.   ¶ ___

5. T F   Fair-trade goods are usually sold door-to-door.   ¶ ___

6. T F   Cooperatives benefit producers because they can pool their resources and afford expensive equipment.   ¶ ___

7. T F   Retailers benefit from fair trade because they get a constant supply of quality products.   ¶ ___

8. T F Retailers decide whether or not a product is certified as fair trade. ¶ ____

9. T F It is fairly easy to determine the price of agricultural products, but it is more difficult for handicrafts. ¶ ____

B. Reread paragraphs 13–15, and highlight or take notes to answer the questions.

1. Ten Thousand Villages has certain benefits for producers. What are they?

   _____

   _____

2. What are some of the challenges for fair trade in developing countries?

   _____

   _____

3. What statistics show that consumers can help lift people out of poverty by buying fair-trade products? _____

VOCABULARY

Vocabulary Building

Read the underlined word or expression in its context and match it with the correct meaning. Use a dictionary if necessary.

____ 1. Many workers who grow products <u>certified as</u> fair trade . . . (¶3)

____ 2. . . . dealing with intermediaries who take a <u>disproportionate</u> share of the revenue . . . (¶4)

____ 3. She . . . <u>launched</u> what would become Ten Thousand Villages. . . . (¶6)

____ 4. They <u>traverse</u> dirt roads. . . . (¶7)

____ 5. . . . the company has inked <u>deals</u> with 60 stores in the San Francisco area. . . . (¶8)

____ 6. . . . buyers are able to . . . develop a <u>sustainable</u> supply chain. (¶10)

____ 7. To <u>verify</u> that the farmers and artisans get a fair-trade price . . . (¶11)

____ 8. . . . the company chooses crafts that <u>reinforce</u> cultural traditions. . . . (¶13)

a. business agreements

b. able to continue for a long time

c. make stronger

d. promised or guaranteed to be

e. started

f. check, make sure

g. too large

h. travel over

Multiword Expressions

Being able to recognize multiword expressions as units is an important reading skill. For each definition below, scan the indicated paragraph to find the equivalent multiword expression and write it on the line.

Definition   **Multiword Expression**

1. extra after paying bills (¶3)   _____

2. registered on a cash register, sold (¶6)   _____

3. enough money to live a decent life on (¶11) _____

4. getting an idea for (¶12 and ¶13)   _____

5. assume they have something without   _____
   thinking about it (¶14)

Vocabulary Review

Complete the following statements about the reading selection with the correct word or expression from the list below. Use each word or expression only once.

certified   left over   straightforward
disproportionate   living wage   sustainable
enable

1. The concept of fair trade is really quite _____.

2. The point is to _____ farmers and artisans to get the best price for their products by eliminating as many intermediaries or middlemen as possible.

3. When intermediaries get a(n) _____ amount of the profit, the producer has almost nothing _____.

4. By forming cooperatives, eliminating middlemen, and reinvesting in the business, co-op members can have a(n) _____ business that provides them with a(n) _____ and raises their standard of living.

5. As a consumer, you can help by buying _____ fair-trade products.

TEXT ANALYSIS *Paragraph Topics*

Reread or skim the selection. Match each paragraph or set of paragraphs with the correct topic.

___ 1. (¶1–2)

___ 2. (¶3–4)

___ 3. (¶5–8)

___ 4. (¶9–10)

___ 5. (¶11–13)

___ 6. (¶14)

___ 7. (¶15)

a. the basic benefits of fair trade and how fair trade is different from previous conditions

b. certification and pricing of fair-trade goods

c. some difficulties of working in the fair-trade system

d. how fair trade got started and two current examples

e. how fair trade functions

f. some benefits of working in the fair-trade system

g. an introduction with an example of what fair trade can do

RESPONDING TO READING **Discuss these questions.**

1. What are the advantages of cooperatives? What are the disadvantages, if any? Explain.

2. What is your opinion of buying fair-trade goods?

3. Do you prefer to buy from small or big businesses? Why?

4. Capitalism can help people escape poverty through fair trade and microlending. On the other hand, capitalism allows businesses to become so big that small businesses can't compete. Has this happened in your area? What, if anything, should be done to allow small businesses to survive?

5. Consumers typically want to pay the lowest price possible. Has this article changed your thinking? Explain.

"VIP, A Conversation" by Harry Newman, Jr., is from *Behind Pinstripes*. More recently it appeared in *The Poetry of Business Life: An Anthology*, edited by Ralph Windle (1994).

BEFORE YOU READ

Thinking about the Topic

Discuss these questions.

1. VIP stands for *very important person*. Who are some VIPs in the business world?
2. Who are some quite ordinary people that VIPs might have a conversation with?

Before you read, turn to Comprehension Check, First Reading, on page 135. Your purpose for the first reading is to be able to answer those questions.

READ

VIP, A Conversation

By Harry Newman, Jr.

1   I have to be there at four thirty
    For a business appointment
    Before a dinner meeting;
    So please step on it¹.

2   *What do you do, if I may ask?*
    He asked.

3   I develop shopping centers
    Small ones, big ones with malls.

4   *Oh you must really be important.*

5   Well, I don't know about that.
    How long is your shift²?

6   *You're my last fare³,*
    I started just before noon.

7   What do you do the rest of the time?

8   *Oh, I go home; only a small place*
    Overlooking the river,
    Work my vegetable garden,
    Go fishing or sailing,
    Sometimes I sit and read
    Or look at the mountains.

9   *I just make enough to get along.*
    That's why it's so nice
    To meet a successful person
    Like you.

---

¹**step on it** *move fast (informal) (it = the gas pedal)*
²**shift** *a work period, usually eight hours*
³**fare** *a passenger in a taxi; fare is also payment for transportation*

First Reading

Answer these questions.

1. Where does this conversation take place? What words in the poem support your answer?

   _____

2. Who are the participants?

   _____

Second Reading

Read the poem at least one more time. Then read each statement below and circle the word that indicates your opinion. Support your response with evidence from the poem. Discuss your answers with your classmates. You probably will not all have the same interpretation.

1. The passenger is the VIP.

   Agree   Neutral   Disagree

   Evidence: _____

2. The taxi driver is more likely to own his own business than the passenger.

   Agree   Neutral   Disagree

   Evidence: _____

3. The taxi driver thinks of himself as an important person.

   Agree   Neutral   Disagree

   Evidence: _____

4. The taxi driver is more polite than the passenger.

   Agree   Neutral   Disagree

   Evidence: _____

5. The passenger is prouder of his/her work than the taxi driver.

   Agree   Neutral   Disagree

   Evidence: _____

6. The passenger is a happy person.

   Agree   Neutral   Disagree

   Evidence: _____

7. The taxi driver is a happy person.

   Agree   Neutral   Disagree

   Evidence: _____

Format of a Poem

Answer these questions.

1. How does the layout of this poem indicate that it is a conversation? Note that there are no quotation marks.
2. The taxi driver is speaking in the sections numbered 8 and 9. Why do you think his comments are divided into two sections?
3. Prepare to read this poem aloud with a partner. One of you will be the VIP, and the other will be the taxi driver. The way you read your part of the poem will depend on how you answered the questions in the Comprehension Check.

RESPONDING TO READING

Discuss these questions.

1. Who is this poem more about, the passenger or the taxi driver?
2. What statement does the poem make about different types of work?

UNIT WRAP-UP

Extending Your Vocabulary

Word Families

Study the chart below to learn other forms of some of the words in this unit. If there is a box with a dash, either there is no word to fill it or the word is missing because it is not one you need to know now.

	NOUNS	VERBS	ADJECTIVES	ADVERBS
1.	competition	compete	competitive	competitively
2.	distribution distributor	distribute	—	—
3.	donation donor	donate	—	—
4.	establishment	establish	—	—
5.	funding	fund	—	—
6.	investment investor	invest reinvest	—	—
7.	innovation innovator	innovate	innovative	—

	NOUNS	VERBS	ADJECTIVES	ADVERBS
8.	management manager	manage	managerial	—
9.	mechanic mechanism	mechanize	mechanical	mechanically
10.	volunteer volunteerism	volunteer	voluntary	voluntarily

For each item below, look at the row in the chart above with the same number. Choose the word that correctly completes the sentence. Be sure it is in the correct form.

1. New businesses with good start-up capital have a _____ advantage.

2. Students sometimes _____ advertising flyers to make money.

3. Learning to _____ to charitable organizations was part of Flannery's upbringing.

4. In referring to a business, you might hear someone say, "That is a well-run _____."

5. We hope to start a small business. We are now looking for _____ for the venture.

6. When you _____ money, you hope to make a profit. Owning a business and buying stocks in someone else's business are two kinds of _____.

7. Some people are _____; they come up with new ideas fairly easily. Their _____ are sometimes good and sometimes kind of crazy.

8. My sister is a _____. She studied _____ at the university and developed good _____ skills.

9. Fair trade allows cooperative farms to _____ production using tractors and other _____ equipment.

10. When people donate their services _____, they are called _____.

Collocations

Learning collocations is one way to improve your vocabulary. Study the chart.

administer (v.)	**administer** a company, grants, a hospital, loans, tests, a program, a school
earn (v.)	**earn** a grade, a living, a living wage, money, a privilege, respect
invest (v.)	**invest** effort, energy, money, resources, time
raise (v.)	**raise** capital, children, funds, goats, money, prices, rates, salary, vegetables, wages
venture (n.)	business, collaborative, commercial, cooperative, joint, **venture**

Complete the sentences below with appropriate collocations. Look at the chart above for help. There may be more than one correct collocation for some sentences.

1. I studied business administration; now I administer a _____.

2. I work in a bank and administer _____.

3. Fair trade helps poor people earn a decent _____ so they can take care of their families.

4. Young people need jobs so they can earn their own _____.

5. You have to earn people's _____. You can't buy it.

6. We invested a great deal of _____ in the project, but not much money.

7. Small businesses often raise _____ by borrowing from banks.

8. If a business raises _____ too much, customers will go elsewhere.

9. It is not easy for single parents to raise their _____ alone.

10. _____ ventures can be good business deals, but they require that people know how to work together well.

**WRITING**

Choose one of the suggestions for writing below. Talk about what you plan to write about with a classmate who chose the same topic. Then follow the instructions for writing.

1. Write three or four questions about one of the following topics. Work with a partner.
   - his or her desire to have a business some day
   - his or her Internet use
   - his or her most important hobby or free-time activity

   Interview your partner, take notes on his or her answers to your questions, and write a short report of your interview using the article "I, Lender" as a model.

2. Imagine you are either the entrepreneur or the taxi driver in the poem "VIP, A Conversation." Write a description of your work life, talking about what it is like to be an entrepreneur or an employee.

3. Read the information in the study skill box. Then review the appropriate reading for each question that follows. Take notes to answer each question, then write your answer in complete sentences, using your notes as a guide.

STUDY SKILL: ANSWERING ESSAY EXAM QUESTIONS

Writing successful short answers to essay exam questions is a valuable skill to develop. Each answer should

  a. answer the question directly and completely without any unrelated information.
  b. be written in complete sentences in your own words.

Teachers sometimes give a list of possible questions before the test. In this case, you have time to review each reading and take notes to remind yourself of what you want to write. If the teacher doesn't give a list, ask yourself questions that you think will be on the test and take notes to answer them.

---

  a. What is the difference between a product and a service?
  b. What does it mean to add value to a resource? Explain with at least one specific example.
  c. What is the difference between a large and a small business? Which type is more common?
  d. What is the role of competition in the free-enterprise system? How does competition benefit the consumer?
  e. What is profit, and what does it indicate about a business?
  f. How do lenders in the developed world help entrepreneurs in the developing world through Kiva.org?
  g. How does the fair-trade system help farmers and artisans in the developing world?

Try to use some of this vocabulary, as well as words in the glossary, in writing about the topic you choose: *a living wage, certified, come up with, competition, deal, dignified, eliminate, enable, establish, evaluate, eventually, get a shot at, get overlooked, initially, invest (reinvest), launch, left over, motivating, ongoing, regulations, rewarding, shift, take for granted, verify, volunteer.*

Business Glossary

audit to check that financial records are correct; this is done by an **auditor**

bond a document promising that a government or company will pay back money it has borrowed, usually with interest

business the buying and selling of goods or services in order to make a profit

buyer a person whose job is to choose and buy goods for a store or company

capital money or property owned or used in business; **operating capital** money available to keep a business going; **start-up capital** money that needs to be spent before a new business or product starts to produce any income; also called the "original investment" in a business

capitalism an economic system in which people are free to start their own businesses by raising capital from other sources and/or using their own capital

competition when two or more companies try to get the same customers or markets; competition generally results in lower prices and higher-quality goods and services for consumers

cooperative a business organization owned equally by all the people working there

corporation a legal entity composed of stockholders that has the right to buy and sell possessions and is legally responsible for its actions

debt capital a way to finance a business in which lenders get interest payments and repayment of the amount they lend within a specified time

distributor an individual or company that gets or supplies goods to stores or companies so they can be sold

economy the system by which a country's money and goods are produced and used (e.g., a capitalist economy)

economics the study of the way in which money and goods are produced and used

employee someone who earns a living by working for someone else's business; the amount they earn is limited to salary, bonuses, and stock options

entrepreneur a person who starts his/her own business and takes risks in order to make a profit

exports products sent to other countries to be sold in those countries

fair trade socially responsible international trade in which poor farmers and producers form cooperatives and receive fair prices for their goods and produce by trading more directly with buyers

financing borrowing money to start, operate, or expand a business

free-enterprise system an economic system in which anyone is free to start a business

free-trade zone an area or situation in which the goods coming into and going out of a country are not taxed

goods things that are produced in order to be sold

imports products brought into a country from other countries to be sold

invest to spend money in a way that you believe will give you a profit or successful result in the future

microlending lending small amounts of money to people who do not qualify for traditional bank loans

middleman an intermediary, someone who buys things in order to make a profit by selling them to someone else

portfolio a collection of stocks and bonds in different companies owned by one person or one company

product something tangible (that can be touched) that exists in nature or is made by people

product development designing and improving a product

productivity the rate at which goods are produced and the amount produced

profit the difference between the amount of money coming in and the amount required to pay the bills

retail the sale of goods in stores to people for their own use as opposed to wholesale, which is the selling of goods in large quantities to retail stores

resource something that can be used to increase wealth (e.g., coal, wood, petroleum); **scarce resource** a resource that costs money, also a resource that is hard to obtain

revenue money that a business or organization receives, especially from selling goods or services

service giving something intangible, such as time, skills, or expertise, in exchange for money

stock options opportunities for employees to buy stock in the company that they work for at a lower price; a stock is a share in the ownership of a corporation

supplier a person or company that provides a particular product

tariffs taxes on imports to make them more expensive than domestic products

venture business activities that involve risk

wares things that are for sale, usually not in a store

yield the amount of something that is produced, also the return on an investment

Finding Your Way

Discuss

1. What abilities do the people in the pictures above need to have in order to be successful in their professions? Which job do you think requires the most intelligence?
2. What is intelligence? What does it mean to say that some people are more intelligent than others?
3. How can understanding our abilities and the ways we are intelligent help us in making career or lifestyle choices?

> *If you enjoy what you do, you'll never work another day in your life.*
>
> Confucius

> *Happiness, or feeling satisfied with life, is unrelated to health, age, money, or most of the other things we'd expect. What really matters is working hard and achieving a goal in an area that challenges you, no matter what your level of accomplishment or walk of life.*
>
> Gilbert Brim, *Ambition: How We Manage Success and Failure Throughout Our Lives*

ABOUT THE READING

"The Foundations of the Theory of Multiple Intelligences" comes from Thomas Armstrong's book *Multiple Intelligences in the Classroom, 2nd edition.* In it, Armstrong presents some of psychologist Howard Gardner's ideas about multiple intelligences and offers ways teachers can apply his theory in the classroom.

Howard Gardner, a professor at the Harvard Graduate School of Education, published his groundbreaking theory of multiple intelligences in *Frames of Mind.*

BEFORE YOU READ

Thinking about the Topic

Discuss these questions.

1. What subjects do you find easiest and most difficult in school?
2. What do you enjoy doing in your free time? What special abilities or intelligence do these activities require?
3. What types of people do you consider intelligent?

Previewing

The title of this selection contains difficult words. Read the dictionary entries, and then answer the questions that follow.

> **foun·da·tion** /faʊnˈdeɪʃən/ *n.* a basic idea, principle, situation, etc. that something develops from SYN **base:** *Reading, writing, and arithmetic provide* **a solid foundation** *for a child's education.* | *The Chinese diet is* **built on a foundation of** *rice, with only small amounts of meat.*

> **the·o·ry** /ˈθɪri/ *n.* an idea or set of ideas that is intended to explain something about life or the world, especially one that has not been proven to be true

1. Read the title and the two section headings. Which section will contain the following types of information?

    a. support for the idea of multiple intelligences _____

    b. definitions of the intelligences _____

2. The word *intelligences* is used in a new way in this selection; you will learn about this new use of *intelligences* as you read. Scan the names of the intelligences and look at the diagram on page 145. Does anything about these eight intelligences surprise you? If so, what?

Before you read, turn to Comprehension Check, First Reading, on page 146. Your purpose for the first reading is to be able to answer those questions.

The Foundations of the Theory of Multiple Intelligences

By Thomas Armstrong

1   In 1904, the minister of public instruction in Paris asked the French psychologist Alfred Binet and a group of colleagues to develop a means of determining which primary grade students were "at risk" for failure so these students could receive remedial attention. Out of their efforts came the first intelligence tests. Imported to the United States several years later, intelligence testing became **widespread**, as did the notion that there was something called "intelligence" that could be objectively measured and reduced to a single number or "IQ"[1] score.

2   Almost eighty years after the first intelligence tests were developed, a Harvard psychologist named Howard Gardner challenged this commonly held belief. Saying that our culture had defined intelligence too narrowly, he proposed in the book *Frames of Mind* (Gardner, 1983) the existence of at least seven basic intelligences. More recently, he has added an eighth. In his theory of multiple intelligences (MI theory), Gardner wanted to broaden our understanding of human potential beyond the confines of the IQ score. . . . He suggested that intelligence has more to do with the **capacity** for (1) solving problems and (2) creating products in a context-rich and naturalistic setting.[2]

THE EIGHT INTELLIGENCES DESCRIBED

3   *Linguistic Intelligence:* The capacity to use words effectively, whether orally (e.g., as a storyteller, orator, or politician) or in writing (e.g., as a poet, playwright, editor, or journalist).

4   *Logical-Mathematical Intelligence:* The capacity to use numbers effectively (e.g., as a mathematician, tax accountant, or statistician) and to reason well (e.g., as a scientist, computer programmer, or logician).

5   *Spatial Intelligence:* The ability to perceive the visual-spatial world accurately (e.g., as a hunter, scout, or guide) and to **transform** those perceptions (e.g., as an interior decorator, architect, artist, or inventor). This intelligence includes sensitivity to color, line, shape, form, space, and the relationships that exist between these elements.

6   *Bodily-Kinesthetic Intelligence:* Expertise in using one's whole body to express ideas and feelings (e.g., as an actor, a mime, athlete, or a dancer) and ability to use one's hands to produce or transform things (e.g., as a craftsperson, sculptor, mechanic, or surgeon).

7   *Musical Intelligence:* The ability to perceive (e.g., as a music aficionado),[3] discriminate (e.g., as a music critic), transform (e.g., as a composer), and express (e.g., as a performer) musical forms.

8   *Interpersonal Intelligence:* Sensitivity to the moods, intentions, motivations, and feelings of other people. This can include sensitivity to facial expressions, voice and gestures; the capacity for discriminating among many different kinds of interpersonal cues; and the ability to respond effectively to those cues.

widespread
a. common
b. unusual

capacity
a. ability
b. big city

transform
a. change
b. remove

---

[1]**IQ** *intelligence quotient, a measure of a person's intelligence*
[2]**context-rich and naturalistic setting** *a place in real life, not a classroom or testing situation*
[3]**aficionado** *a lover or fan of something (from Spanish)*

9   *Intrapersonal Intelligence:* Self-knowledge and the ability to act adaptively on the basis of that knowledge. This intelligence includes having an accurate picture of oneself (one's strengths and limitations); awareness of inner moods, intentions, motivations, temperaments, and desires; and the capacity for self-discipline, self-understanding, and self-esteem.

10   *Naturalist Intelligence:* Expertise in the recognition and classification of the numerous species[4]—the flora and fauna—of an individual's environment. This also includes sensitivity to other natural phenomena (e.g., cloud formations and mountains) and, in the case of those

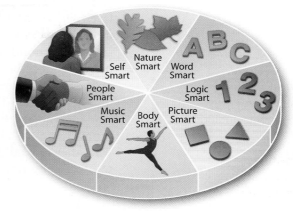

growing up in an urban environment, the capacity to discriminate among nonliving forms such as cars, sneakers, and music CD covers.

THE THEORETICAL BASIS FOR MI THEORY

11   Many people look at the eight categories—particularly musical, spatial, and bodily-kinesthetic—and wonder why Howard Gardner insists on calling them intelligences, not *talents* or *aptitudes*. Gardner realized that many people are used to hearing expressions like "He's not very intelligent, but he has a wonderful aptitude for music," thus, he was quite conscious of his use of the word *intelligence* to describe each category. He said in an interview that he wanted to make people think and talk about the idea of intelligences. If he had said that there are eight kinds of **competencies**, people would have yawned and said, "Yeah, yeah." But by calling them "intelligences," he was saying that we have tended to put on a pedestal one variety called intelligence, and there are actually several of them, and some are things we have never thought of as "intelligence" at all.

12   Gardner set up certain basic "tests" that each intelligence had to meet to be considered a **full-fledged** intelligence and not simply a talent, skill, or aptitude. Two of the tests follow.

Potential Isolation by Brain Damage

13   At the Boston Veterans Administration, he worked with individuals who had suffered accidents or illnesses that affected only specific areas of the brain. For example, a person with a lesion[5] in Broca's area (left frontal lobe) might have a **substantial portion** of his linguistic intelligence damaged, and thus experience great difficulty speaking, reading, and writing. Yet he might still be able to sing, do math, dance, **reflect on** feelings, and relate to others. A person with a lesion in the temporal lobe of the right hemisphere might have her musical capacities **impaired**, while frontal lobe lesions might primarily affect the personal intelligences.

(continued)

---

[4]**species** *a group of animals (fauna) or plants (flora) of the same kind that can breed with each other*
[5]**lesion** *a wound or injury*

competencies
a. abilities
b. competitions

full-fledged
a. hungry
b. complete

substantial portion
a. large part
b. small part

reflect on
a. forget about
b. think about

impaired
a. damaged
b. doubled

The Existence of Savants, Prodigies, and Other Exceptional Individuals

14   Gardner suggests that in some people we can see single intelligences operating at high levels. Savants are individuals who demonstrate superior abilities in . . . one intelligence while their other intelligences function at a low level. They seem to exist for each of the eight intelligences. For instance, in the movie *Rain Man* (which is based on a true story), Dustin Hoffman plays the role of Raymond, a logical-mathematical savant. Raymond rapidly calculates multidigit numbers in his head and does other amazing mathematical feats, yet he has poor peer relationships, low language functioning, and a lack of **insight** into his own life. There are also savants who draw exceptionally well, savants who have amazing musical memories (e.g., playing a composition after hearing it only one time), savants who read complex material yet don't comprehend what they're reading (hyperlexics), and savants who have exceptional sensitivity to nature or animals.

insight
a. ability
b. understanding

COMPREHENSION CHECK

First Reading

Answer these questions.

1. Why does Gardner use the word *intelligences*?
   a. He wants people to understand what he is talking about.
   b. He wants people to change their definition of intelligence.
   c. He thinks it is easier to understand than similar words.

2. What are the eight intelligences? Match the name of each intelligence on the left with an ability on the right.

    ____ 1. linguistic
    ____ 2. logical-mathematical
    ____ 3. spatial
    ____ 4. bodily-kinesthetic
    ____ 5. musical
    ____ 6. interpersonal
    ____ 7. intrapersonal
    ____ 8. naturalist

a. ability to understand and get along with other people
b. ability to classify plants, animals, rocks
c. ability with numbers, clear thinking
d. ability to understand yourself
e. ability with language
f. ability in singing, playing an instrument
g. ability with color, line, space
h. ability in using the parts of one's body

Second Reading

Read the selection again. Mark the statements *T* (true) or *F* (false). Write the paragraph number(s) where you found evidence for each answer.

1. T F Gardner believes that IQ tests are a good measure of human intelligence. ¶ ____

2. T F Giving students opportunities to write is the only way to develop their linguistic intelligence. ¶ ____

3. T F A computer programmer has to have strong interpersonal intelligence. ¶ ____

4. T F A painter or sculptor needs both spatial and bodily-kinesthetic intelligence. ¶ ____

5. T F To have musical intelligence, a person has to be able to play an instrument. ¶ ____

6. T F A person with good interpersonal intelligence makes a good team member. ¶ ____

7. T F People with strong intrapersonal intelligence know themselves but cannot change. ¶ ____

8. T F People with well-developed naturalist intelligence are good at classifying things. ¶ ____

9. T F Gardner found that when a part of the brain is damaged, certain intelligences are affected but not others. ¶ ____

10. T F A savant who has high logical-mathematical intelligence but little inter- or intrapersonal intelligence is support for Gardner's theory that human intelligences are separate. ¶ ____

Vocabulary Building

Read the underlined word or expression in its context and match it with the correct meaning. Use a dictionary if necessary.

PART 1

____ 1. . . . so these students could receive <u>remedial</u> attention.(¶1)

____ 2. . . . as did the <u>notion</u> that there was something called "intelligence" . . . (¶1)

____ 3. <u>Logical</u>-Mathematical Intelligence (¶4)

____ 4. The capacity . . . to <u>reason</u> well . . . (¶4)

____ 5. The ability to <u>perceive</u> the visual-spatial world accurately . . . (¶5)

____ 6. . . . perceive the visual-spatial world <u>accurately</u> . . . (¶5)

____ 7. <u>Expertise</u> in using one's whole body . . . (¶6)

a. correctly

b. think logically

c. idea

d. special skill or knowledge learned by experience or training

e. related to logic, the science of thinking carefully

f. intended to provide improvement in something

g. see

PART 2

____ 8. Sensitivity to the <u>moods</u>, intentions, motivations, and feelings of other people. (¶8)

____ 9. . . . <u>intentions</u>, . . . and feelings of other people. (¶8)

____10. . . . <u>motivations</u>, and feelings of other people. (¶8)

____11. . . . the capacity for <u>self-discipline</u>, self-understanding, and self-esteem. (¶9)

____12. . . . the capacity for self-discipline, self-understanding, and <u>self-esteem</u>. (¶9)

____13. . . . . the numerous species—the flora and fauna—of an individual's <u>environment</u>. (¶10)

____14. . . . growing up in an <u>urban</u> environment . . . (¶10)

h. the ability to make yourself do the things you ought to do without being told to

i. natural world or situation around you

j. feeling that you have value as a person

k. ways people feel at a particular time

l. relating to a town or city

m. what people plan to do

n. reasons a person does something

Using a Dictionary

Write the number for the dictionary entry below that best defines the underlined word as it is used in the sentence.

1. . . . to broaden our understanding of human <u>potential</u> . . . (¶2)

   Definition # _____

   > **po·ten·tial** /pəˈtɛnʃəl/ *n.* [U] **1** the possibility that something will develop in a certain way, or have a particular effect: +for *There is some potential for abuse in the system.* | +of *We need to explore the potential of this idea further.* | have the potential to do sth *The planned bombing had the potential to kill and injure many people.* **2** a natural ability or quality that could develop to make a person or thing very good: *This room has potential.* | *a young singer with potential* | the potential to do sth *The country shows the potential to be a global economic leader.* | sb's potential as sth *In his third year he is finally showing his great potential as a golfer.* | achieve/reach/realize your (full) potential (=succeed in doing as well as you possibly can)

2. . . . and the relationships that exist between these <u>elements.</u> (¶5)

   Definition # _____

   > **el·e·ment** /ˈɛləmənt/ *n.* [C]
   >
   > **1 PART** one part or feature of a whole system, plan, piece of work etc., especially one that is basic or important: +of *Vegetables are a vital element of the human diet.* | +in *Religion was an element in the dispute.* | *The movie has all the elements of a great love story.*
   >
   > **2 PEOPLE** USUALLY DISAPPROVING a group of people who can be recognized by particular behavior or beliefs: *The clubs also tend to attract a criminal element* (=people who do illegal things).
   >
   > **3 CHEMISTRY** CHEMISTRY a substance that consists of only one type of atom and which cannot be changed into a simpler substance. CARBON gold and oxygen are elements. → see also COMPOUND: *chemical elements*
   >
   > **4 THE ELEMENTS** weather, especially bad weather: *The tent was their only protection from the elements.*

3. The ability to . . . <u>discriminate</u> (e.g., as a music critic) . . . musical forms. (¶7)

   Definition # _____

   > **dis·crim·i·nate** /dɪˈskrɪməˌneɪt/ *v.* **1** [I] to treat a person or a group differently from another in an unfair way: +against *The policies discriminate against disabled people.* | +in *discrimination in hiring* | discriminate on the grounds/basis of sth *It was found that the company discriminated on the grounds of race.* | *Employers may not discriminate in favor of* (=give better treatment to) *younger applicants.* **2** [I,T] to recognize a difference between things SYN differentiate: +between *Young babies can discriminate between pleasant and unpleasant odors.* | discriminate sth from sth *You need to learn to discriminate fact from opinion.* [Origin: 1600–1700 Latin *discriminare* to divide, from *discernere* to separate]

4. . . . the ability or capacity for discriminating among many different kinds of interpersonal <u>cues</u> . . . (¶8)

Definition # _____

> **cue** /kyu/ *n.* [C] **1** an action or event that is a signal for something else to happen *some people can cope with hearing loss by using other cues to meaning.* **2** a word or action that is a signal for someone to speak or act in a play, movie, etc. : *She stood nervously in the wings waiting for her cue.* **3** *on cue* happening or done at exactly the right moment **4** *take your cue from sb* to use someone else's actions or behavior to show you what you should do or how you should behave.

5. . . . why Howard Gardner <u>insists</u> on calling them intelligences not *talents* or *aptitudes.* (¶11)

Definition # _____

> **in·sist** /ɪnˈsɪst/ *v.* [I,T] **1** to say firmly and often that something is true, especially when other people think it may not be true: insist (that) *Mike insisted that he was right.* | *Experts insist there is no chance of a recession in the near future.* | insist on sth *She has always insisted on her innocence.* **2** to demand that something should happen and refuse to let anyone say "no": *Let me pay this time. I insist* (=used to firmly and politely offer to do something). | insist (that) *I'm glad my parents insisted that we speak Spanish at home.* | *Bud insisted he drive us home.* | insist on (sb) doing sth *He insisted on going with me.*

6. . . . we have tended to <u>put on a pedestal</u> one variety called intelligence . . . (¶11)

Definition # _____

> **ped·es·tal** /ˈpɛdəstl/ *n.* **1** the base that you put a STATUE or a PILLAR on **2** *put sb/sth on a pedestal* to admire someone or something too much because you think s/he or it is perfect

Vocabulary Review

Complete the following statements about the reading selection with the correct word or expression from the list below. Use each word or expression only once.

accurate	logical	reason
cues	motivations	theory
impairs	perceive	transform

1. Over many years, Howard Gardner developed his _____ of multiple intelligences.

2. Gardner knew that when people say someone is intelligent, they mean the person is "school smart"—good at reading, math, and _____ thinking.

3. But people have other intelligences in addition to the ability to _____ well.

4. For example, spatial intelligence is the ability to _____ the physical world accurately.

5. Sculptors, mechanics, and surgeons have bodily-kinesthetic intelligence; they use their hands to produce or _____ things.

6. People with interpersonal intelligence can perceive the moods and _____ of other people. They can understand these and other interpersonal _____ and respond to them effectively.

7. If you have good intrapersonal intelligence, you have a(n) _____ understanding of yourself.

8. MI theory is supported by evidence that damage to the brain _____ one intelligence but not another.

TEXT ANALYSIS   *Brief Examples*

> The letters "e.g." are an abbreviation for the Latin words *exempli gratia,* meaning "for example." They are often used to mark short examples. The brief examples in this selection all serve the same purpose. If you understand one or two of the words in each set, you will probably understand the kind of intelligence being described. If you are curious about the other examples, list the ones you and your classmates don't know and share the work of finding them in a dictionary.

Answer these questions.

1. What kind of brief examples does Armstrong give to help you understand the different intelligences? Why are the examples he chooses appropriate for each intelligence?
2. What punctuation convention does the writer use to separate the examples from the text?

RESPONDING TO READING

Discuss these questions.

1. Schools generally emphasize the linguistic and logical-mathematical intelligences. Think about the schools you have attended. How good have they been in developing all eight intelligences in students?

2. How well developed are your own eight intelligences? List the eight intelligences on a piece of paper. Evaluate each of your intelligences using this scale: 3 = strong, 2 = moderate, 1 = weak.

Multiple Intelligences Inventory*

Step 1: Respond to this inventory individually. Check the statements that apply to you in each intelligence category.

LINGUISTIC INTELLIGENCE

_____ I enjoy reading books, magazines, and websites.

_____ I enjoy word games and word puzzles.

_____ Social studies, history, and my native language class were easier for me in school than math and science.

_____ When I drive down a highway, I pay more attention to the words written on billboards than to the scenery.

_____ I like talking about my ideas and often refer to things that I have read or heard about.

LOGICAL-MATHEMATICAL INTELLIGENCE

_____ Math and/or science were among my favorite subjects in school, and I am interested in developments in science.

_____ I enjoy playing games or solving problems that require logical thinking such as number puzzles and chess.

_____ I sometimes think in abstract, wordless, imageless ideas.

_____ I like finding logical errors in things people say or do (this doesn't mean being negative).

_____ If something breaks or won't work, I look at the pieces and try to figure out how it works and how to fix it.

SPATIAL INTELLIGENCE

_____ I often see clear visual images when I close my eyes.

_____ I pay attention to shape and color.

_____ I enjoy doing jigsaw puzzles and other visual puzzles.

_____ I'm good at reading maps, charts, graphs, and other diagrams.

_____ I enjoy hobbies such as drawing, painting, and photography.

BODILY-KINESTHETIC INTELLIGENCE

_____ I play at least one sport or do some physical activity on a regular basis.

_____ I find it difficult to sit still for long periods of time.

_____ I enjoy working with my hands and with tools.

_____ I learn better by doing something than by reading about it.

_____ I like to dance.

MUSICAL INTELLIGENCE

_____ I frequently listen to music.

_____ I play a musical instrument.

_____ I can easily keep time to a piece of music and can move to a musical beat.

_____ I know the tunes (melodies) to many different songs or musical pieces.

_____ I often have a tune running through my mind.

INTERPERSONAL INTELLIGENCE

_____ I'm the sort of person that people come to for advice.

_____ I would rather work in a group than alone.

_____ I have close friends who are important to me.

_____ I like to belong to clubs and organizations.

_____ I would rather spend my evenings at a party or with friends than stay at home alone.

INTRAPERSONAL INTELLIGENCE

_____ I regularly spend time alone meditating, reflecting, or thinking about important life questions.

_____ I can respond to problems in life without too much difficulty.

_____ I have a clear idea of who I am and what my strengths and weaknesses are.

_____ I have personal goals which I think about often.

_____ I have a special hobby or interest that I usually do alone.

NATURALIST INTELLIGENCE

_____ I am very aware of my surroundings.

_____ I like to collect and organize or categorize things like rocks, flowers, insects, or stamps.

_____ I am quite good at discriminating between different species of flora and fauna.

_____ Environmental issues are important to me.

_____ I like activities like hiking, camping, and gardening.

Step 2: If you checked three or more items in a category, you are probably quite strong in that intelligence. Which of your intelligences are the strongest? Which are the weakest? Compare the results of this inventory with your self-evaluation from Responding to Reading on page 151.

This inventory is a shortened composite of several (including Armstrong's) with slight modifications in vocabulary for the L2 reader.

CHAPTER 22

ABOUT THE READING

"Styles of Thinking and Learning" is an excerpt from an article by psychologist Robert Sternberg, dean of arts and sciences at Tufts University. The article was published in the professional journal *Language Testing*.

BEFORE YOU READ

Thinking about the Topic

Discuss these questions.

In Chapter 21, Armstrong gives examples of careers that are *compatible* with, or match, different intelligences. These careers are *a good fit* for people with these intelligences.

1. What type of work or career would be a good fit for the following people?
   - a person who likes to be active
   - a person who likes to plan and organize things
   - a person who does not like to follow instructions
2. What type of work or career would be a bad fit for these people?

Previewing

Read the title, the first paragraph, the first sentence of paragraphs 2–9, and the last paragraph. Then answer these questions.

1. Are styles and abilities the same thing?

2. Which of the following facts about Alex, Bill, and Curt did you learn from your preview?

   ___ a. Curt, Alex, and Bill had similar abilities.

   ___ b. Alex was a good student.

   ___ c. Bill became a scientist.

   ___ d. Curt's job was compatible with his style of thinking.

3. Which idea will the writer illustrate, using Alex, Bill, and Curt as examples?

   a. People have different abilities and different styles.

   b. People can have similar abilities but different styles.

Before you read, turn to Comprehension Check, First Reading, on page 156. Your purpose for the first reading is to be able to answer those questions.

Styles of Thinking and Learning
By Robert Sternberg

identical
a. different
b. the same

1   A style is a way of thinking. It is not an ability, but rather how we use the abilities we have. We do not have a style, but rather a profile of styles. People may be almost **identical** in their abilities, and yet have very different styles. Consider, for example, three friends: Alex, Bill and Curt (who are real people—only the names are changed).

2   Alex was a model student all the way through his senior year at a highly prestigious college and received outstanding grades. The first time he had academic problems was when he was in his senior year of college. For the first time, he had to really think for himself. Up to then, he had been able to get As by doing what the teachers told him to do. But his senior essay was an independent project, and now he found himself **at a loss**. He was fine so long as other people told him what to do, but was in trouble when he had to come up with his own ideas. He probably could have come up with his own ideas if he really wanted to: he just didn't like doing it and didn't feel comfortable doing things differently from others. So he was smart and able, just so long as there was someone to guide him.

at a loss
a. knowing what to do
b. not knowing what to do

3   Alex had thought about being a historian or possibly a writer. He certainly had the ability to follow either of those careers. But his style of thinking was much **better suited to** the career he actually chose: today he is a contracts lawyer and a highly successful one. When people ask him what he does, he describes his work as directed by others. Investment bankers[1] decide on a deal and then instruct Alex to draw up a contract. Thus, the bankers set the structure and Alex works within it. But if the bankers decide to modify their deal, they have to pay Alex to do it. So every time they have an idea or change one, they have to pay Alex. He has found a job that is a good fit for his style of thinking. The important thing to remember is that Alex had the ability to do a lot of things, but found a career that was a good fit to the way he likes to use his abilities. As a result, he is happy with his career.

better suited to
a. more appropriate for
b. better dressed for

4   Alex is also happy in his personal life, which in many ways is compatible with his professional life. Alex and his wife have 2.5 children (well, three actually), and live in a comfortable suburb in a major metropolitan area. They keep up with the Joneses[2] and take their cues in their life from what others do. They do not question much why they do what they do, but rather fall into the patterns set for them by others.

5   Bill matched Alex in abilities, but not in school achievement. Bill's primary style is quite different from Alex's, and is one that schools don't usually reward. Most schools value an Alex, the bright child who does what he or she is told; fewer value a Bill, a child who is bright but who wants to do things his or her own way. Indeed, children like Bill are often seen as behavior problems, or as **lacking in** ability.

lacking in
a. not having
b. having

6   Bill's experience was the opposite of Alex's. He got a mediocre grade in his introductory science course. He came into his own when he could work independently and come up with his own ideas. He first began to feel successful when he started his career as a research scientist. As a scientist, he was in a position to come up with his own ideas—his own theories, his own experiments. He no longer had to follow the instructions of a teacher or supervisor.

(continued)

---

[1]**investment bankers** *bankers who specialize in using money to make money*
[2]**keep up with the Joneses** *to do or have what one's neighbors do or have*

dissatisfied
a. happy
b. not happy

predominant
a. most important
b. least important

scores of
a. a few
b. many

7   Bill's personal life has also showed his style of thinking. Bill's first marriage, to the "right" woman from the "right" background, ended in divorce. The marriage was a model of what society says a marriage should be, but Bill was extremely bored. He had the right house in the right neighborhood with the right schools, and his wife thought he was crazy to be **dissatisfied**. In his second marriage, however, Bill lives the kind of life that he prefers, in the wrong neighborhood with the wrong spouse, and he is happier than ever before. He's doing it his way, which is what he always wanted.

8   Curt was similar in abilities to Alex and Bill, but his **predominant** style was different. As a college student, he was editor of the college-course critique,[3] and as a result was in charge of evaluating every course taught at the college. When he went out on dates, he even gave his dates a test of values—which they did not know they were taking. If they passed the test, he continued to go out with them; if not, that was the end of the relationship. Today, Curt is in his mid-40s and, perhaps predictably, is still not married.

9   But Curt, like Alex and Bill, has found a job that is a good fit to his predominant style of thinking. Curt always liked to evaluate people and things, and today he is a highly successful psychotherapist[4] who evaluates people and their problems and prescribes courses of therapy for them. Curt had the ability to do many things, but he found a job that was compatible with his style.

10   Alex, Bill, and Curt are the lucky ones. But go to any high school or college reunion,[5] and you will meet **scores of** people who went into the wrong job for them. Perhaps they did what their guidance or career counselor told them to do, based on abilities or even interests, but many of them are in careers where they feel they are at a dead end.[6] People often feel at a dead end when the work they do isn't a good fit with the best uses of their talents. Understanding styles can help people better understand why some activities fit them and others do not, and even why some people fit them and others do not.

---

[3]**college-course critique** *a pamphlet in which students evaluate the courses at their college or university*
[4]**psychotherapist** *a doctor of medicine who treats mental and emotional problems*
[5]**high school or college reunion** *a party where graduates get together years after they have graduated*
[6]**dead end** *the end of a road that goes nowhere*

COMPREHENSION CHECK

First Reading

Complete the statements with the person's occupation and predominant, or most common, style of thinking or working.

1. Alex is a successful _____.

    He is good at _____.

2. Bill is a successful _____.

    He is good at _____.

3. Curt is a successful _____.

    He is good at _____.

Second Reading

Read the selection again. Match the beginning of each sentence on the left with the correct reason on the right to form a complete sentence.

___ 1. Alex had trouble with his senior project . . .

___ 2. Alex is happy as a contracts lawyer . . .

___ 3. Bill felt successful as a research scientist . . .

___ 4. Curt has probably not married . . .

___ 5. Alex, Bill, and Curt are the lucky ones . . .

___ 6. Many people feel at a dead end in their work . . .

___ 7. Understanding your profile of styles is important . . .

a. because he is always evaluating people and finding something wrong with them.

b. because it may help you choose the right lifestyle and partner.

c. because he is good at following the instructions of the people who hire him.

d. because each went into the correct job for his style of thinking.

e. because he had to think independently, and that wasn't his style.

f. because he could think independently and use his own ideas.

g. because they have jobs that don't fit their styles of thinking.

VOCABULARY

Vocabulary Building

Read the underlined word or expression in its context, and match it with the correct meaning. Use a dictionary if necessary.

___ 1. We do not have a style, but rather a <u>profile</u> of styles. (¶1)

___ 2. . . . he had to <u>come up with</u> his own ideas. (¶2)

___ 3. . . . he is a <u>contracts</u> lawyer and a highly successful one. (¶3)

___ 4. Investment bankers decide on a <u>deal</u>. . . . (¶3)

___ 5. But if the bankers decide to <u>modify</u> their deal . . . (¶3)

___ 6. . . . (a style) that schools don't usually <u>reward.</u> (¶5)

___ 7. (Bill) got a <u>mediocre</u> grade in his introductory science course. (¶6)

___ 8. The marriage was a <u>model</u> of what society says a marriage should be. . . . (¶7)

a. value, give good grades to

b. legal written agreements between people, companies, etc.

c. agreement, especially in business or politics

d. perfect example

e. neither good nor bad

f. set of details that together describe someone or something

g. think of

h. change

Synonyms

As you know, synonyms are words that have the same or almost the same meaning. However, their meanings usually differ slightly and they collocate (go together) with different words.

For example, *same* and *identical* are synonyms.

a. We have the *same / identical* classes.
b. We say *identical* twins, but not *same* twins.

Be aware that you cannot always substitute a synonym for a word and have the exact same meaning.

Read the underlined word or expression in its context. Circle the two choices that are similar in meaning in this context. Use a dictionary if necessary.

1. Alex was a <u>model</u> student. . . . (¶2)

   a. excellent   b. very good   c. terrible

2. . . . at a highly <u>prestigious</u> college . . . (¶2)

   a. unknown   b. famous   c. respected

3. . . . and received <u>outstanding</u> grades. (¶2)

   a. excellent   b. superior   c. low

4. . . . (they) instruct Alex to <u>draw up</u> a contract. (¶3)

   a. prepare   b. modify   c. write

5. He has found a job that is <u>a good fit for</u> his style of thinking. (¶3)

   a. suited to   b. compatible with   c. unlike

6. . . . his personal life . . . is compatible with his <u>professional life.</u> (¶4)

   a. marriage   b. work   c. career

7. Bill's <u>primary</u> style is quite different from Alex's. . . . (¶5)

   a. predominant   b. least important   c. major

8. . . . a child who is <u>bright</u> . . . (¶5)

   a. lazy   b. intelligent   c. smart

9. He <u>came into his own</u>. . . . (¶6)

   a. found his true abilities   b. had a lot of belongings   c. found his own way

10. Curt . . . was <u>in charge of</u> evaluating every course . . . (¶8)

   a. responsible for   b. in control of   c. paying money for

Vocabulary Review

Complete the following statements about the reading selection with the correct word or expression from the list below. Use each word or expression only once.

at a loss	come up with	contracts	model
came into his own	compatible	evaluate	styles

1. Robert Sternberg illustrates personal _____ by describing the academic, professional, and personal lives of three men.

2. Alex was a(n) _____ student, but he found himself _____ when he had to do an independent project in his senior year.

3. Alex became a lawyer who draws up _____ for investment bankers because he prefers to have his work directed by others.

4. Bill is just the opposite. Bill didn't do well in his early science courses, but he _____ when he could work independently.

5. He is a research scientist and likes his work because he has to _____ his own theories.

6. Curt is happy as a psychotherapist because he likes to _____ people and their problems.

7. Alex, Bill, and Curt are lucky because their jobs are _____ with their personal styles.

TEXT ANALYSIS   *Extended Examples*

The writer of this selection chose to give quite a few details about Alex, Bill, and Curt, making this reading a long, or extended example. Answer the questions about the reading.

1. Why do you think the writer thought a longer example was needed? (Hint: Reread the definition of *style* he gives in paragraph 1.)

2. What three categories of details does the writer give about each man?

3. What does the writer want to illustrate with these details?

RESPONDING TO READING

Discuss these questions.

1. What are some other personal styles people have? Add more personal styles to the list below. What jobs are compatible with these personal styles? Write them in the chart.

Other Personal Styles	Compatible Jobs
likes to work on a conventional 9–5 schedule	
likes to work with details	

2. Which have you experienced: schools that value students who do what they are told, or schools that help students follow their own ways? What are the advantages and disadvantages of each?

"No Job Is Beneath You" is from *Ten Things I Wish I'd Known—Before I Went Out into the Real World* by Maria Shriver. Shriver belongs to a prominent American family; her uncle, John F. Kennedy, was the thirty-fifth president of the United States. Shriver's book grew out of a university graduation speech that she gave.

BEFORE YOU READ

Thinking about the Topic

Discuss these questions.

1. What are some things that can make a first job difficult?
2. What attitude will probably help you succeed at your first job?

Previewing

Read the title and first two paragraphs of this selection, and answer the questions.

1. What do the title and paragraph 1 suggest will be Shriver's message in this selection?
2. Why do some college graduates need to hear this message?

Before you read, turn to Comprehension Check, First Reading, on page 163. Your purpose for the first reading is to be able to answer those questions.

READ

acquaintances
a. your pets
b. people you know

stunning
a. surprising
b. boring

No Job Is Beneath You *By Maria Shriver*

1   Parents, friends, and **acquaintances** may regularly tell you you're smarter than Bill Gates[1] and can do anything you want. But I don't know anyone who hasn't benefited from a willingness to start at the bottom. Even Bill Gates began by doing odd jobs as a programmer.

2   Starting at the bottom builds character. It makes you hungry and determined. It's also a very good way to find out, **stunning** as it may be, that you're not as smart as you think you are. And it's the best way to LEARN. Because if you haven't figured it out already, let me clue you in: There's a lot more to learn out there. And you can learn it only by admitting that you don't know it already, which means starting at the bottom. Which is where I started. Many times.

3   At the end of college, I focused on making my dream a reality. I applied to the Westinghouse broadcast training program—sort of a glorified internship program[2] for the TV stations the company owned around the country. I was accepted into the program, and right out of school headed off to KYW-TV in Philadelphia for my first job in television. Starting salary in the glamorous world of TV news: $12,000. I arrived in the newsroom bright-eyed, bushy-tailed, with a spanking new degree in American studies, and naïve. Very naïve.

(continued)

---

[1]**Bill Gates** *the founder of Microsoft® and a wealthy philanthropist*
[2]**glorified internship program** *a little better than the usual internship program that gives work experience to young people starting their career*

veteran
a. experienced
   employee
b. inexperienced
   employee

amuse themselves
a. have fun
b. work hard

last
a. follow
b. stay long

interloper
a. insider
b. outsider

nasty
a. nice
b. mean

scoured
a. searched
b. cleaned

tips and leads
a. ideas for stories
b. famous people

4   I introduced myself to the news director, the guy who ran the station's news operation. In many ways, I have yet to recover. He was a local news **veteran**. He was tough, smart, opinionated, and determined to let me know immediately that HIS newsroom was NOT a place for rich little dilettantes like ME to **amuse themselves** until they got married. He wasn't quite sure how many strings I pulled to get this job that fifty deserving kids were DYING to get, but I was taking up space, and don't think that he was happy about it. He explained to me that he didn't want and couldn't afford anyone in the newsroom who wasn't serious, who wasn't willing to work twenty-four hours a day, eight days a week, holidays included, night shifts, morning shifts—and how about a DOUBLE shift? He didn't need some twenty-one-year-old graduate from a fancy college—RICH kid at that—coming in there thinking, "Oooooh, fun! Can I play with the cameras, too? Hey, I wanna go on the air!"

5   He spoke to me like no one ever had spoken to me. And he didn't care, because he was quite sure that I wouldn't **last** and would be gone from there before anyone ever noticed I'd arrived—because I was a STRANGER, an **INTERLOPER**, and didn't belong in the hard-driving, hard-hitting, hard-boiled world of TV news, like HE did. And don't you forget it, you spoiled brat.

6   Wham-bam—hello? I walked out of his office, down the hall to the bathroom, locked myself in a stall, and cried my eyes out. That was the first and last time I ever cried at work. (Not the last time I ever cried *about* work. Just the last time I cried *at* work.) . . .

7   I'm sure that news director wanted to break me. But instead, he helped make me. Because after I blew my nose and came out of the bathroom—and, I must admit, called my parents to tell them what the **nasty** man said to me—I set out to prove him wrong.

8   There was nothing I wouldn't do in the newsroom. I worked my tail off. Dawn patrol, graveyard shift.³ Double shift? Yes, please. I worked weekdays, holidays, weekends, days and days on end. I worked wherever I could in the newsroom, because I didn't have my own desk. I **scoured** the wire services⁴ for stories for other people to do. I worked the assignment desk at 4 A.M. Listened to police scanners for hours to get **tips and leads**. Worked the phones checking out stories and setting up shoots. I logged⁵ the real reporters' videotapes so they wouldn't have to. I answered the phones on the first ring. And I made the news director's darn coffee! And even smiled about it. This was *my* journalism school, and I constructed my own curriculum by finding out what no one else wanted to do and doing it.

9   You see, what the news director didn't recognize was that TV news was my *passion*. I wasn't at KYW to play around or get married or become famous. I was there for one reason only: to begin pursuing that passion. And this guy was indirectly fueling it by challenging it. He made me ask myself that very first day whether I could take the heat. Could I keep my eye on the prize down the road? Did I have a fire in my belly? Because you need that conviction if you're going to be able to brush off criticism and negativity dished out by guys like that. And I knew he wouldn't be the last. So he bruised my ego, so what? I'll *use* him. I'll *learn* from him. I'll *show* him. And I did.

10   You know, maybe he was right. Maybe I was a brat. When what I want is out of reach, I keep climbing until I get it. I've had that kind of determination since I was a kid. And when you work hard to pull yourself up, it really means something when you get there. . . . You can't short-circuit the learning process. It takes time to get to the top, and that's good—because by the time you get there, you'll have learned what you need to know to stay there.

---

³**dawn patrol, graveyard shift** *slang for very early and very late hours*
⁴**wire services** *agencies that provide news stories and photos electronically (e.g., Associated Press)*
⁵**logged** *wrote down information about the tapes in a log, or record book*

First Reading

Answer these questions.

1. What was Shriver's first job?
2. What kind of welcome did her boss give her? How did she react to it?

Second Reading

Read the selection again. Highlight or take notes to answer the questions.

1. What are Shriver's good reasons for starting at the bottom? (¶2)

   _____

   _____

   _____

   _____

   _____

2. What kind of people didn't the news director want working in his newsroom? (¶4)

   _____

   _____

   _____

   _____

   _____

3. What was Shriver willing to do to get ahead in the hard-hitting career of news reporting? (¶8)

   _____

   _____

   _____

   _____

   _____

Vocabulary Building

Read the underlined word or expression in its context and match it with the correct meaning. Use a dictionary if necessary.

___ 1. I arrived in the newsroom . . . with a spanking new degree in American studies . . . and <u>naïve</u>. (¶3)

___ 2. . . . I have yet to <u>recover</u>. (¶4)

___ 3. (The boss) was <u>tough</u>, smart, opinionated . . . (¶4)

___ 4. . . . HIS newsroom was NOT a place for rich little <u>dilettantes</u> like ME . . . (¶4)

___ 5. And don't you forget it, you <u>spoiled brat</u>. (¶5)

___ 6. This was *my* journalism school, and I constructed my own <u>curriculum</u> . . . (¶8)

___ 7. . . . TV news was my *passion*. (¶9)

___ 8. I was there for one reason only: to begin <u>pursuing</u> that passion. (¶9)

___ 9. . . . you need that <u>conviction</u> if you're going to be able to brush off criticism . . . (¶9)

___ 10. . . . you need that conviction if you're going to be able to brush off <u>criticism</u> . . . (¶9)

a. program of study

b. strong belief, determination

c. strong liking for something

d. following

e. someone interested in a subject or activity but not really serious about it

f. negative remarks or comments

g. inexperienced, unrealistically optimistic

h. badly behaved child, often child of rich parents who gave her everything

i. get back to a former condition

j. strict, not easy to deal with

Idioms

An *idiom* is an expression that has a special meaning that is not clear from the individual words in the expression. Idioms are not always in the dictionary, so before looking up an idiom, try to infer its meaning from the context.

Some idioms have one or two words that help you understand at least part of the meaning.

Example 1: But I don't know anyone who hasn't benefited from a willingness to *start at the bottom*. (¶1)

The word *bottom* gives you help in inferring that this idiom means *start in the lowest-level job*.

Example 2: He wasn't quite sure how many *strings I pulled* to get this job. . . . (¶4)

The words *pull strings* do not give you much help with the meaning. This idiom means to use influence—who you know (contacts)—to get something you want.

Read the underlined idiom in its context. Match it with the correct meaning.

____ 1. I arrived in the newsroom <u>bright-eyed, bushy-tailed</u> . . . (¶3)

____ 2. . . . this job that fifty deserving kids <u>were DYING to get</u> . . . (¶4)

____ 3. . . . but I was <u>taking up space</u> . . . (¶4)

____ 4. I'm sure that news director wanted to <u>break me</u>. But instead, he helped <u>make me</u>. (¶7) (usually *make you or break you*)

____ 5. I <u>worked my tail off</u>. (¶8)

____ 6. He made me ask myself . . . whether I could <u>take the heat</u>. (¶9)

____ 7. Could I <u>keep my eye on the prize</u> down the road? (¶9)

____ 8. Could I keep my eye on the prize <u>down the road</u>? (¶9)

____ 9. Did I have <u>a fire in my belly</u>? (¶9)

___10. So he <u>bruised my ego</u>, so what? (¶9)

___11. . . . work hard to <u>pull yourself up</u> . . . (¶10)

a. destroy your will, make you succeed

b. in the future

c. passion

d. wide awake and ready to go

e. hurt my feelings

f. survive the difficulties

g. make progress, get better jobs

h. wanted passionately

i. filling the position (of a more deserving person)

j. worked very hard

k. focus on the reward

Vocabulary Review

Complete the following statements about the reading selection with the correct word or expression from the list below. Use each word or expression only once.

bruised her ego	naïve	pulled strings	spoiled brats
criticism	passion	pursued	take the heat

1. Maria Shriver had one _____ in life—to become a TV news reporter and anchorwoman.

2. On the first day of her new job, her boss, the director of the newsroom, made it very difficult for her. He told her that he thought she had _____ to get the job.

3. He said he didn't want any _____ in the newsroom who were just playing around until they got married.

4. Maria was _____; she didn't have much work experience, and no one had ever talked to her like that.

5. The boss may have _____, but after a good cry in the bathroom, she decided to accept his _____ and negativity as a challenge. She decided to prove that she could _____.

6. Shriver did every job, no matter how low, and learned everything she could as she _____ her career in the TV news business.

Informal and Formal Language: Paraphrasing

> *Paraphrasing* is saying or expressing an idea using different words with the same meaning.
>
> We paraphrase regularly in speaking. When someone asks us what another person said, we almost never quote the person's exact words. We use our own words, which is paraphrasing.
>
> Paraphrasing can change statements from formal to informal or vice versa, depending on the words chosen.

Read the underlined word or phrase in its context. Then scan the paragraph in the reading for an informal expression that means the same thing. Write it on the line.

1. . . . let me <u>tell you</u>. . . . (¶2)

   _____

2. I . . . <u>went</u> to KYW-TV in Philadelphia. . . . (¶3)

   _____

3. . . . <u>began, started</u> to prove him wrong. (¶7)

   _____

4. . . . worked the phones checking out stories and <u>arranging photography sessions</u>. (¶8)

   _____

5. I wasn't at KYW to <u>waste time</u> or get married or become famous. (¶9)

   _____

6. And this guy was indirectly <u>encouraging, increasing</u> (my passion) by challenging it. (¶9)

   _____

7. . . . you need that conviction if you're going to be able to <u>pay no attention to</u> criticism. . . . (¶9)

   _____

8. . . . criticism and negativity <u>given, spoken</u> by guys like that. (¶9)

   _____

RESPONDING TO READING

Discuss these questions.

1. Why do you think the news director was so hard on Shriver that first day?

2. Do you know what you want to do at this stage of your life? If so, what is it? Do you think it will change or not? Explain.

3. If you have worked, share stories about jobs you have had. Think about what you were required to do, your reaction to the work, how people treated you, and what you learned.

ABOUT THE READING

This selection by Robert Fulghum (1937–) is from his third book, *Uh Oh: Some Observations from Both Sides of the Refrigerator Door,* published in 1991. In his short essays, Robert Fulghum expresses his thoughts about the ordinary things that have happened to him in his life as a father, grandfather, neighbor, cowboy, minister, and many other roles. Fulghum is a musician, painter, sculptor, and writer, a man of many intelligences. His best-selling books have been translated into twenty-seven languages.

BEFORE YOU READ

Thinking about the Topic

Discuss these questions.

1. What kind of person were you when you were about five years old?
2. What did you like to do?
3. How did the world look to you?

Previewing

MAKING PREDICTIONS

While reading, efficient readers form ideas and make predictions about what is coming next. As they read, they check to see if their predictions are correct. If they are not correct, they make changes in their ideas and continue reading.

1. Read the first sentence of the selection. Which is the better prediction? Why?

   a. Fulghum will write only about young children.

   b. Fulghum will write about young children and young adults.

2. Read the second and third sentences. What will follow?

   a. examples of similarities between kindergartens and colleges

   b. examples of differences between kindergartens and colleges

3. Read to the end of the paragraph. What will follow?

   a. examples of how kindergarten children and college students are similar

   b. examples of how kindergarten children and college students are different

Before you read, turn to Comprehension Check, First Reading, on page 168. Your purpose for the first reading is to be able to answer those questions.

Untitled *By Robert Fulghum*

1   Over the last couple of years I have been a frequent guest in schools; most often invited by kindergartens and colleges. The environments differ only **in scale**. In the beginners' classroom and on university campuses the same opportunities and facilities exist. Tools for reading and writing are there—words and numbers; areas **devoted to** scientific experiment—labs[1] and work boxes; and those things necessary for the arts—paint, music, costumes, room to dance—likewise present and available. In kindergarten, however, the resources are in one room, with access for all. In college, the resources are in separate buildings, with limited availability. But the most **apparent** difference is in the self-image of the students.

2   Ask a kindergarten class, "How many of you can draw?" and all hands shoot up. Yes, of course we can draw—all of us. What can you draw? Anything! How about a dog eating a fire truck in a jungle? Sure! How big do you want it?

3   How many of you can sing? All hands. Of course we sing! What can you sing? Anything! What if you don't know the words? No problem, we make them up. Let's sing! Now? Why not!

4   How many of you dance? **Unanimous** again. What kind of music do you like to dance to? Any kind! Let's dance! Now? Sure, why not?

5   Do you like to act in plays? Yes! Do you play musical instruments? Yes! Do you write poetry? Yes! Can you read and write and count? Yes! We're learning that stuff now.

6   Their answer is Yes! Over and over again, Yes! The children are confident in spirit, infinite in resources,[2] and eager to learn. Everything is still possible.

7   Try those same questions on a college audience. A small percentage of the students will raise their hands when asked if they draw or dance or sing or paint or act or play an instrument. Not infrequently, those who do raise their hands will want to qualify their response with their limitations: "I only play piano, I only draw horses, I only dance to rock and roll, I only sing in the shower."

8   When asked why the limitations, college students answer they do not have talent, are not majoring in the subject, or have not done any of these things since about third grade, or worse, that they are embarrassed for others to see them sing or dance or act. You can imagine the response to the same questions asked of an older audience. The answer: No, none of the above.

9   What went wrong between kindergarten and college?

10   What happened to YES! of course I can?

---

[1]**labs** *short for* laboratories
[2]**infinite in resources** *resourceful, unlimited in what one can do*

First Reading

Answer these questions.

1. What difference does Fulghum see between kindergarten children and college students?
2. What does Fulghum want to know at the end of the selection?

Second Reading

Read the selection again, and answer the questions.

1. Which of the following words and expressions apply to kindergartners (mark these *K*), and which apply to college students (mark these *C*)?

_____ Anything!

_____ not majoring in the subject

_____ confident in spirit

_____ eager to learn

_____ embarrassed

_____ have not done any of these things since about third grade

_____ No problem!

_____ Of course!

_____ qualify responses with their limitations

_____ Sure, why not?

_____ they do not have talent

_____ Yes!

2. Which is the best statement of the main idea of this selection?
   a. Kindergarteners and college students have the same facilities and opportunities.
   b. College students have lost the enthusiasm and self-confidence that they had as kindergartners.
   c. College students are more easily embarrassed than kindergarteners.

VOCABULARY

Vocabulary Building

Read the underlined word or expression in its context and match it with the correct meaning. Use a dictionary if necessary.

____ 1. . . . the same opportunities and <u>facilities</u> exist. (¶1)

____ 2. . . . the <u>resources</u> are in one room, with access for all. (¶1)

____ 3. . . . the resources are in one room, with <u>access</u> for all. (¶1)

____ 4. But the most apparent difference is in the <u>self-image</u> of the students. (¶1)

____ 5. No problem, we <u>make</u> them <u>up</u>. (¶3)

____ 6. The children are <u>confident</u> in spirit. . . . (¶6)

____ 7. . . . those who do raise their hands will want to <u>qualify</u> their response with their limitations. . . . (¶7)

____ 8. . . . college students answer they do not have talent, are not <u>majoring in</u> the subject . . . (¶8)

a. the way they see themselves

b. studying as their main subject

c. sure they can do something well

d. space and equipment provided for a special purpose

e. limit, narrow

f. chance or right to use something, availability

g. invent

h. materials that are available to use

Vocabulary Review

Complete the following statements about the reading selection with the correct word or expression from the list below. Use each word or expression only once.

access	confident	facilities	qualify
apparent	embarrassed	make up	self-image

1. According to Fulghum, kindergarteners and college students have

   _____ to similar _____ and resources,

   but he sees a big difference between the two groups.

2. The most _____ difference is in the way they view

   themselves, their _____.

3. Little kids are full of enthusiasm and self-confidence; older people are often

   _____ about doing things that they think they can't do well.

4. Young children are imaginative and will _____ the words

   to a song if they don't know them all.

5. College students usually _____ their abilities with the

   word *only*—"I only sing in the shower."

6. Fulghum seems to wish that college students could be as _____

   as kindergarteners.

TEXT ANALYSIS

Using Exact Words

In paragraphs 2–5, Fulghum shows the self-image of children by giving their responses to his questions instead of telling us about them. For example, he doesn't say, "The children were very enthusiastic." Instead he uses their exact words: "Yes! We can!"

Divide a piece of paper into two columns. On the left, list the questions Fulghum asks the children. On the right, write the children's answers. Paragraph 2 is done as an example. Do the same thing for paragraphs 3–5.

Fulghum's Questions (¶2)	Children's Answers
How many of you can draw?	Yes, of course we can draw—all of us.
What can you draw?	Anything!
How about a dog eating a fire truck in a jungle?	Sure! How big do you want it?

Study the children's answers. Which of their words, in your opinion, show the following characteristics? Write them on the line.

1. They are positive about their abilities.

   _____

2. They see no limitations.

_____

3. They are imaginative and creative.

_____

RESPONDING TO READING

Discuss these questions.

1. What title would you give to this selection? Explain.

2. Fulghum asks, "What went wrong between kindergarten and college? What happened to _Yes! of course I can_?" Based on your own experience, is this a good question to ask? If so, what do you think the answer to his question is?

3. Fulghum is concerned that people lose confidence in their abilities, and lose enthusiasm and creativity as they grow older. What value might these characteristics have for adults in terms of their career and life choices?

UNIT WRAP-UP

Extending Your Vocabulary

Word Families

Study the chart below to learn other forms of some of the words in this unit. If there is a box with a dash, either there is no word to fill it or the word is missing because it is not one you need to know now.

	NOUNS	VERBS	ADJECTIVES	ADVERBS
1.	accuracy	—	accurate	accurately
2.	criticism	criticize	critical	critically
3.	intention	intend	intentional unintentional	intentionally unintentionally
4.	modification	modify	modified unmodified	—
5.	motivation	motivate	motivated unmotivated	—
6.	logic logician	—	logical	logically
7.	passion	—	passionate	passionately
8.	perception	perceive	perceptive	—
9.	prestige	—	prestigious	—
10.	pursuit	pursue	—	—

For each item below, look at the row in the chart on page 171 with the same number. Choose the word that correctly completes the sentence. Be sure it is in the correct form.

1. When students write compositions, part of the grade is often for grammatical
_____.

2. Some people are very _____ of other people. They
_____ everything they do.

3. I didn't _____ to hurt your feelings. I'm sorry. It was
completely _____.

4. The engineer suggested some _____ in the plan.

5. It takes a lot to _____ me, but I am very
_____ to do well on this job.

6. If you are interested in a career as a lawyer, you have to learn to think
_____.

7. My sister is _____ about her work at the Children's
Hospital.

8. People with high interpersonal intelligence are _____
when it comes to understanding other people.

9. Many people are not interested in the _____ that comes
with being president of a company.

10. The United States Declaration of Independence says that people have a right
to "life, liberty, and the _____ of happiness."

Words with More Than One Meaning

Read each sentence. Match the underlined word or expression with the correct meaning. In some cases, you will use the same answer twice. An asterisk indicates a meaning that was used in this unit.

1. ___ The bankers decided to modify
their deal.*

___ They don't have a great deal of money.

___ OK, it's a deal.

___ It's your turn to deal. Use these cards.

___ I got a good deal on my used car.

___ Do you have to make such a big deal
about winning?

a. agreement, especially in
business or politics

b. said when making an
agreement

c. give out playing cards

d. large quantity of something

e. talk about it so much

f. price

2. ____ I am quite good at <u>discriminating</u>*
small differences in color.

____ The news editor <u>discriminated</u> against
Shriver because she came from a rich
family.

a. treat a person or group
differently in an unfair way

b. recognize a difference
between things

3. ____ The <u>environment</u>* in kindergarten is
not that different from the environment
in college, according to Fulghum.

____ I am very concerned about what
people are doing to the <u>environment</u>.

____ I wish we had a more pleasant
<u>environment</u> at work.

a. the land, water, and air in
which living things exist

b. the general situation,
including people,
facilities, and rules

4. ____ No problem, we <u>make</u> them <u>up</u>.*

____ Young people <u>make up</u> about
50 percent of migrants.

____ I missed a test which I have to <u>make up</u>
this week.

____ My friend and I <u>made up</u> quickly after
our silly disagreement.

a. add up to, form

b. become friends again

c. invent, imagine

d. do something you didn't do
when it was scheduled

5. ____ Alex was a <u>model</u>* student.

____ The marriage was a <u>model</u>* of what
society says a marriage should be.

____ My son likes to build <u>model</u> airplanes.

____ I have worked as a <u>model</u>.

____ I'm looking for a car, and I've seen lots
of different <u>models</u>. I don't know what
to buy.

a. type or design

b. small copy of something

c. perfect example of
something good

d. someone who wears
clothes to show them or is
employed to be painted or
photographed

6. ____ College students often use *only* to
<u>qualify</u>* their statements about what
they can do.

____ We didn't <u>qualify</u> for the bank loan.

____ My brother <u>qualified</u> for the U.S.
Open tennis tournament.

a. have the requirements for

b. limit, narrow

7. ____ My boss is <u>tough</u>,* smart, and
opinionated.

____ That's a <u>tough</u> neighborhood.

____ This meat is <u>tough</u>.

____ Are you <u>tough</u> enough to take
criticism?

____ It was a <u>tough</u> exam.

a. difficult, hard

b. able to deal with difficult
situations

c. strict, not easy to deal with

d. difficult to cut or eat

e. likely to have or use
violence and crime

WRITING **Choose one of the suggestions for writing below. Talk about what you plan to write with a classmate who chose the same topic. Then follow the instructions for writing.**

1. Describe yourself or a person you know. Include characteristics or styles such as the ones in the list below. To make your description come alive, give specific examples of things the person does and <u>says</u>. The number of paragraphs you write will depend on the number of characteristics you choose and the amount of information you give about each.
   - curious about everything
   - likes to be physically active
   - likes to plan and organize things
   - works well under pressure/works best without pressure
   - likes to work alone/with other people
   - likes/doesn't like routine
   - likes/doesn't like to follow instructions

2. Write one or two paragraphs about either a or b.
   a. If you have not begun your career, write about a type of work or career that you would like to pursue. Use these questions as a guide:
      - What type of work would you like to do in the future?
      - Why will it be a good fit with your abilities or personal styles?
   b. If you are working and happy with your work, explain how your work fits your abilities and styles. If you are not happy in your career, write about a career change you would like to make. Explain why you think it will be better for you.

Try to use some of the following vocabulary in writing about the topic you choose: *be dying to, be suited for, capacity, career, come up with, compatible with, confident, conviction, criticism, embarrassed, environment, in charge of, lack, logical, motivated, naïve, outstanding, passion, prestigious, primary, professional, pursue, qualified for, self-discipline, self-esteem, self-image, set out, take criticism, tough.*

Word List

CHAPTER 1
aimless
apparently*
care about
contented
diminish*
disappoint
give up
hilarious
hug (v.)
humiliation
involve a trauma
jock
kinship
lack (drive)
look out for
maintain*
pray
pressure (n.)
scold
security
slow
take care of
uttered a word of
  reproach

CHAPTER 2
academic* career
academically* oriented*
achievement*
actually
adolescence
alienated (adj.)
analysis*
aspiration
behavior
concerned (about)
conduct* (n.)
contrast* (v.)
crowd (n.)
day-to-day influence on
  schooling
delinquency
delinquent
equivalent*
finding (n.)
influence (n., v.)
peer
pressure (n.)
track (v.)
whether

CHAPTER 3
awkward
blame oneself
bother (v.)
capable* (of)
comment* (on)
disability
find out
get held back
ignore*
keep up
make fun of
mean (adj.)
minor* (adj.)
presume*
put up with
stay away from
stay behind
stick up for
tease (v.)
toddler
weird
willpower

CHAPTER 5
asset
better-off
destination
determined (adj.)
developed countries
developing countries
discrimination*
eager
emigrate
endurance
flexible*
homeland
host country
integrate* (into)
manual* labor*
network*
obstacle
persecution
perseverance
policy*
precarious
qualified (adj.)
racism
resilience
resourcefulness
rewarding (adj.)

seek*
smuggler
xenophobia

CHAPTER 6
ambition
attribute* (v.)
brain drain
contribute* (to)
deserve
destiny
drop out of
empowering (adj.)
enable*
evolve*
impressed (adj.)
initially*
let alone
major* (adj.)
make ends meet
make up for
on the horizon
option*
oversee
shortage (of)
solitude
stuck
tough
vacuum
vicious cycle*
weep/wept

CHAPTER 7
abandon
appeal (n.)
concentration
decent
decline* (n.)
deposit (n.)
depressed* (adj.)
district
ethnic* conflict
forlorn
hard-working
metropolis
newcomer
on welfare
once-bustling
on welfare*
plummet
pool wages

promote*
proportionally
refugee
reputation
revitalize
revival
sagging (adj.)
shrink
shrivel
suburban area
thrift
thriving (adj.)
unexpected
upsurge
work ethic*

CHAPTER 8
articulate (v.)
ashamed
belt out
distinct*
extended dialogues
gossip (n.)
insert* (v.)
left in the dark
longing
lyrics
outsider
persistently* tugging
resonate
signal (v.)
sporadically
transfer* (v.)

CHAPTER 9
accomplish
addict
amazing (adj.)
anxious
break free from
competing (adj.)
complex* (adj.)
complicated (adj.)
concentrate* (v.)
device
doomed to
efficiently
engage in
gadget
keep in touch with
keep (someone/something)
  from

*Words with an asterisk can be found on the Academic Word List as based on the Compleat Lexical Tutor site (Classic Vocabulary Profiler).

obsessive
overuse (v.)
prioritize*
reorient*
sequentially*
simultaneously
solely*
tons of

CHAPTER 10
autonomy
boring (adj.)
coordinate* (v.)
dedication
defray
donate
drastically
equip*
incident*
incredible
miracle
mischief
recipient
recruit (v.)
refurbish
saturate the market
solicit
take for granted*
tragic

CHAPTER 11
ads, advertisements
barrage
capture (v.)
bombard
conventional*
ethnicity*
gender*
get into your head
invasion of privacy
monitor* (n., v.)
opening volley
pop up
privacy invasion
rate (n.)
retailer
surveillance
tactic
target* (v.)
tune it out

CHAPTER 12
anxious
ashamed
at once
cry out for
cut down on
deduce*
purchase* (n.)
range* (of)

ratio* (of)
resist
tidy up
trigger* (v.)
trill (n.)
unique*

CHAPTER 13
average (adj.)
casual
contrary to*
cutoff point
engagement
expect, expectation
lead to
marital satisfaction
optimistic
questionnaire
set (someone) up for
single (adj.)
tough
unrealistically

CHAPTER 14
absolutely
advice
be stuck
be supposed to
bother (v.)
call for
compliment (v.)
cute
embarrassing (adj.)
get in with
get off
go out with
guy
hand down
next generation of
quit
sensitive
sophisticated
stand it
terrific
tradition*

CHAPTER 15
amazed (at)
contact* (n.)
contemporary*
contend with
curiosity
disturbing (adj.)
elaborate (adj.)
enlightening (adj.)
fascinated with (adj.)
fill in the blanks
targeted
initial* (adj.)
issue* (n.)

obsession
prompt (someone) to
savvy
track (v.)
turn up

CHAPTER 16
argue
brag
chance (adj.)
chuckle
courtship
fidget
foolish
give in
grin (n.)
long to
peek (v.)
ploy
release* (v.)
scared (adj.)
scream (v.)
shiver (v.)
short of
sole*
stare (v.)
suspicious
wired (adj.)

CHAPTER 17
barely
business
capital (n.)
capitalism
competition
economics*
economy*
eliminate*
employee
enforce* restrictions*
entrepreneur
evaluate*
eventually*
expertise*
free trade
free enterprise system
impose* trade barriers
initially*
innovative*
motivating* (adj.)
parties (n.)
product
profit (n.)
public
reinvest*
renovate
resource*
reward (n., v.)
scarce resource
service (n.)
shift* (v.)

surface (v.)
tangible/intangible
tariff
undertake*/undertook
venture
voluntary* exchange

CHAPTER 18
contingent on
dignified (adj.)
donor
establish*
fund* (v.)
get overlooked
manage
microlending
pioneer (v.)
portfolio
post (v.)
raise (v.)
shot (n.)
software engineer
sort (v.)
transparent
upbringing
witness (v.)

CHAPTER 19
certified (as)
come up with
concept*
deal (n.)
disproportionate*
enable*
fair trade
launch (n., v.)
left over
living wage
mechanical help
ongoing*
reinforce*
ring up/rang up
straightforward*
sustainable*
table linens
take for granted*
traverse
verify
wares

CHAPTER 21
accurately*
bodily-kinesthetic
capacity *
competencies
cue (n.)
discriminate*
element*
environment*
expertise*

foundation*
full-fledged
impair (v.)
insight*
insist (on)
intelligences
intention*
interpersonal
intrapersonal
linguistic
logical
logical-mathematical
mood
motivation
mustical
naturalist
notion
perceive
potential
put on a pedestal
reason (v.)
reflect on
remedial
self-discipline
self-esteem
spatial
substantial portion*
theory
transform

urban
widespread

CHAPTER 22
a good fit (for)
at a loss
better suited to
bright
come into (one's) own
come up with
compatible*
contract* (n.)
deal (n.)
dissatisfied
draw up
identical*
in charge of
lacking in
mediocre
model (adj., n.)
modify*
outstanding
predominant*
prestigious
primary*
professional* life
profile (n.)
reward (v.)
scores of

CHAPTER 23
acquaintance
amuse
bright-eyed, bushy-tailed
bruise (one's) ego
brush off
clue you in
conviction
criticism
curriculum
dilettante
dish out
down the road
dying to
fire in (one's) belly
fueling (something)
head off to
interloper
keep (one's) eye on the prize
last (v.)
make you or break you
naïve
nasty
passion
play around
pull (one's self) up
pull strings
pursue*
recover*

scour
set out for
set up
spoiled brat
start at the
   bottom
stunning (adj.)
take the heat
take up space
tips and leads
tough
veteran
work (one's) tail off

CHAPTER 24
access* (n.)
apparent*
confident
devoted* to
facilities*
in scale

major in

make up

qualify

resources*

self-image

unanimous

Map of North America

Map of the World

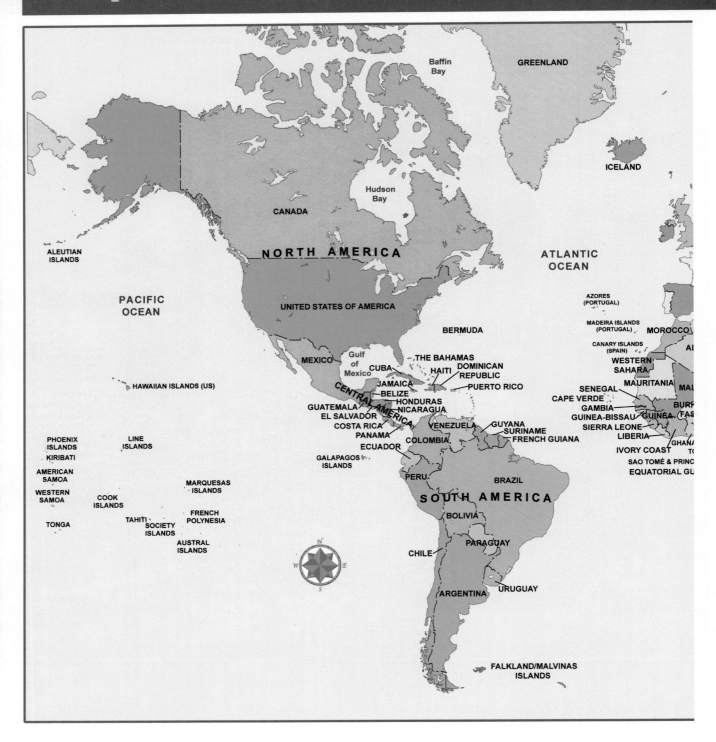

GREENLAND

Baffin Bay

ICELAND

Hudson Bay

CANADA

ALEUTIAN ISLANDS

NORTH AMERICA

ATLANTIC OCEAN

PACIFIC OCEAN

UNITED STATES OF AMERICA

AZORES (PORTUGAL)

BERMUDA

MADEIRA ISLANDS (PORTUGAL)

MOROCCO

MEXICO

Gulf of Mexico

CUBA

THE BAHAMAS

DOMINICAN REPUBLIC

HAITI

CANARY ISLANDS (SPAIN)

WESTERN SAHARA

HAWAIIAN ISLANDS (US)

JAMAICA

PUERTO RICO

MAURITANIA

CENTRAL AMERICA

BELIZE

HONDURAS

SENEGAL

MAL

GUATEMALA

NICARAGUA

CAPE VERDE

BURF

EL SALVADOR

GAMBIA

GUINEA-BISSAU

GUINEA

FAS

COSTA RICA

VENEZUELA

GUYANA

SIERRA LEONE

PHOENIX ISLANDS

LINE ISLANDS

PANAMA

SURINAME

LIBERIA

GHANA

KIRIBATI

ECUADOR

COLOMBIA

FRENCH GUIANA

IVORY COAST

TO

AMERICAN SAMOA

GALAPAGOS ISLANDS

SAO TOMÉ & PRINC

EQUATORIAL GU

WESTERN SAMOA

COOK ISLANDS

MARQUESAS ISLANDS

PERU

BRAZIL

TONGA

TAHITI

FRENCH POLYNESIA

SOUTH AMERICA

SOCIETY ISLANDS

BOLIVIA

AUSTRAL ISLANDS

PARAGUAY

CHILE

ARGENTINA

URUGUAY

FALKLAND/MALVINAS ISLANDS

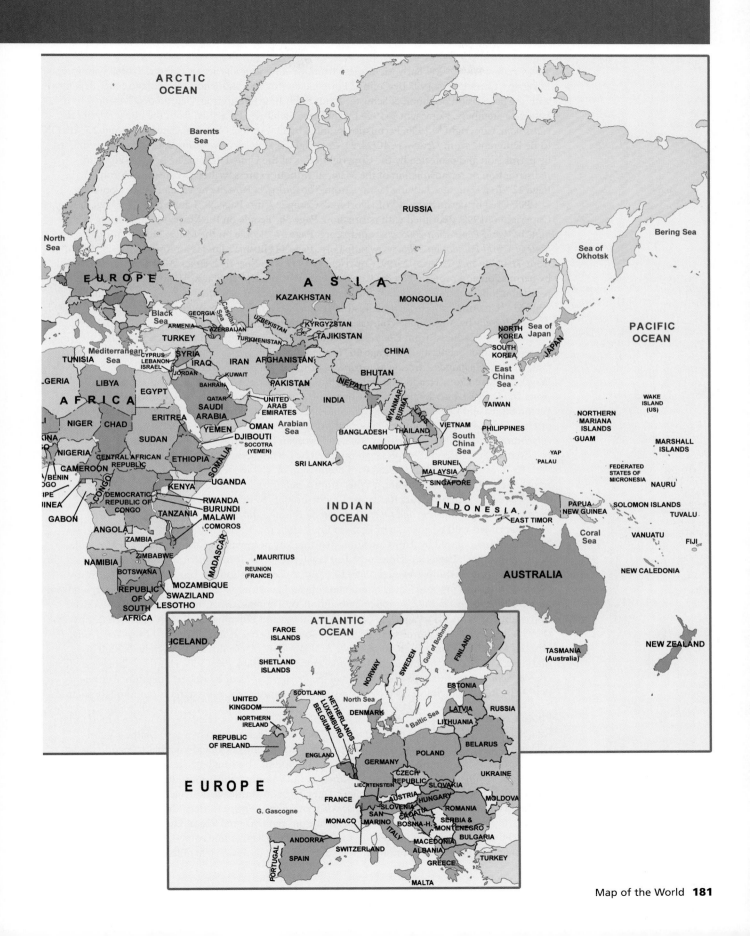

ARCTIC OCEAN

Barents Sea

RUSSIA

North Sea

Bering Sea

Sea of Okhotsk

E U R O P E

A S I A

KAZAKHSTAN

MONGOLIA

Black Sea

GEORGIA

ARMENIA

AZERBAIJAN

UZBEKISTAN

KYRGYZSTAN

TAJIKISTAN

Sea of Japan

PACIFIC OCEAN

TURKEY

TURKMENISTAN

NORTH KOREA

JAPAN

Mediterranean Sea

CYPRUS

LEBANON

ISRAEL

SYRIA

IRAQ

IRAN

AFGHANISTAN

CHINA

SOUTH KOREA

TUNISIA

JORDAN

KUWAIT

BAHRAIN

PAKISTAN

NEPAL

BHUTAN

East China Sea

ALGERIA

LIBYA

EGYPT

QATAR

UNITED ARAB EMIRATES

INDIA

MYANMAR BURMA

TAIWAN

WAKE ISLAND (US)

A F R I C A

SAUDI ARABIA

LAOS

VIETNAM

NORTHERN MARIANA ISLANDS

NIGER

CHAD

ERITREA

OMAN

Arabian Sea

BANGLADESH

THAILAND

PHILIPPINES

GUAM

MARSHALL ISLANDS

YEMEN

DJIBOUTI

SOCOTRA (YEMEN)

CAMBODIA

South China Sea

YAP

PALAU

NIGERIA

CENTRAL AFRICAN REPUBLIC

ETHIOPIA

SRI LANKA

FEDERATED STATES OF MICRONESIA

NAURU

CAMEROON

SOMALIA

UGANDA

BRUNEI

MALAYSIA

SINGAPORE

BENIN

CONGO

KENYA

CONGO

DEMOCRATIC REPUBLIC OF CONGO

RWANDA

BURUNDI

MALAWI

I N D O N E S I A

PAPUA NEW GUINEA

SOLOMON ISLANDS

TUVALU

GUINEA

GABON

TANZANIA

INDIAN OCEAN

EAST TIMOR

VANUATU

FIJI

ANGOLA

COMOROS

ZAMBIA

MADAGASCAR

Coral Sea

NEW CALEDONIA

NAMIBIA

ZIMBABWE

MAURITIUS

BOTSWANA

REUNION (FRANCE)

AUSTRALIA

MOZAMBIQUE

SWAZILAND

REPUBLIC OF SOUTH AFRICA

LESOTHO

TASMANIA (Australia)

NEW ZEALAND

ATLANTIC OCEAN

FAROE ISLANDS

SWEDEN

Gulf of Bothnia

FINLAND

ICELAND

SHETLAND ISLANDS

NORWAY

ESTONIA

RUSSIA

UNITED KINGDOM

SCOTLAND

NETHERLANDS

LUXEMBURG

BELGIUM

North Sea

DENMARK

Baltic Sea

LATVIA

LITHUANIA

NORTHERN IRELAND

REPUBLIC OF IRELAND

ENGLAND

GERMANY

POLAND

BELARUS

UKRAINE

E U R O P E

LIECHTENSTEIN

CZECH REPUBLIC

SLOVAKIA

FRANCE

AUSTRIA

HUNGARY

MOLDOVA

G. Gascogne

SLOVENIA

CROATIA

ROMANIA

SAN MARINO

BOSNIA-H.

SERBIA & MONTENEGRO

BULGARIA

MONACO

ITALY

MACEDONIA

ANDORRA

SWITZERLAND

ALBANIA

PORTUGAL

SPAIN

GREECE

TURKEY

MALTA

Credits

Text Credits: Page 3 "My Early Memories," from *My American Journey* by Colin L. Powell with Joseph E. Persico. Copyright © 1995 by Colin L. Powell. **Page 10** "Peer Influences on Achievement." Reprinted with the permission of Simon & Schuster Adult Publishing Group from *Beyond the Classroom* by Laurence Steinberg. Copyright © 1996 by Laurence Steinberg. Excerpted from the book, *Beyond the Classroom*. Copyright © 1996. Permission granted by Lowenstein-Yost Associated, Inc. **Page 15** "It's OK to Be Different," from *Newsweek* 10/24/94. Copyright © 1994 *Newsweek, Inc.* All rights reserved. Used by permission and protected by the Copyright Laws of the United States. The printing copying redistribution or retransmission of the Material without express written permission is prohibited. **Page 22** "To a Daughter Leaving Home," from *The Imperfect Paradise* by Linda Pastan. Copyright © 1988. Used by permission of W.E. Norton & Company, Inc. **Page 28** "I am a door" by Nagesh Rao. Copyright © 1995. Reprinted with permission. **Page 30** "People on the Move: Moving Young" from *State of World Population 2006*. www.unfpa.org. **Page 37** "People on the Move: Moving Young," from *State of World Population 2006*. www.unfpa.org. **Page 44** "Bosnia's Loss Is an American City's Gain," from *The New York Times*, 4/25/99. Copyright © 1999. *The New York Times*. All rights reserved. Used by permission and protected by the Copyright Laws of the United States. The printing, copying, redistribution, or retransmission of the Material without express written permission is prohibited. **Page 51** "(Un)American" by Patricia Justine Tumang, excerpted from *Waking Up American: Coming of Age Biculturally* by Angela Jane Fountas. Reprinted by permission of Perseus Books Group. **Page 60** "Multitasking Madness" from *Choices*, September 2007. Copyright © 2007 by Scholastic Inc. Reprinted by permission of Scholastic, Inc. **Page 66** "In the Blink of an Eye" by Becky Vaugh from the May 2004 issue of *Lake Highlands Advocate Magazine*. Reprinted with permission. **Page 71** "Advertisers Try New Ways to Get into Your Head," featured on *ABC World News*. Reprinted with permission. **Page 76** "21" from *The Devil's Larder* by Jim Crace. Copyright © 2001 by Jim Crace. Reprinted with permission of Farrar, Straus and Giroux, LLC. **Page 85** "Students Think Love Conquers All." Reprinted by permission of *USA Today*. **Page 90** "Untitled," excerpt from *What Do You Care What Other People Think? Further Adventures of a Curious Character* by Richard Feynman as told to Ralph Leighton. Copyright © 1988 by Gweneth Feynman and Ralph Leighton. Used by permission of W.W. Norton & Company, Inc. **Page 95** "Googling Your Date." Used with permission of The Associated Press. Copyright © 2008. All rights reserved. **Page 100** "Finding a Wife," from *Small Faces* by Gary Soto. Copyright © 1986 by Gary Soto. **Page 114** "Entrepreneurs Recognize Opportunities" by Steve Mariotti, excerpted from *Entrepreneurship—Starting and Operating a Small Business*, 1st edition. Copyright © 2007. Pgs. 3–7, 9–10. Reprinted with permission of Pearson Education, Inc. Upper Saddle River, NJ. **Page 122** "I, Lender." Interviewed by Amy Crawford. Reprinted by permission of the *Smithsonian Magazine*. Copyright © 2007. **Page 128** "How to Be Fair" by Karen Kroll, from *American Way*, 6/15/05. Copyright © 2005. Reprinted with permission. **Page 134** "VIP, A Conversation" by Harry Newman, Jr., from *Behind Pinstripes*. **Page 144** "The Foundations of the Theory of Multiple Intelligences," excerpted from *Multiple Intelligences in the Classroom*, 2nd edition, by Thomas Armstrong. Alexandria, VA. ASCD. Copyright © 2000 ASCD. **Page 155** "Styles of Thinking and Learning" by Robert Sternberg. Copyright © 1995. Reprinted with permission. **Page 161** "No Job Is Beneath You," excerpted from *Ten Things I Wish I'd Known—Before I Went Out into the Real World* by Maria Shriver. Copyright © 2000 by Maria Shriver. Used by permission of Grand Central Publishing. **Page 168** "Untitled," short essay from *Uh Oh: Some Observations from Both Sides of the Refrigerator Door* by Robert Fulghum. Copyright © 1991 by Robert Fulghum. Used by permission of Villard Books, a division of Random House, Inc.

Photo Credits: Cover (top left) Stephen Maka/Photex/Zefa/Corbis, (center right) Dave King/Dorling Kindersley © Weald and Downland Open Air Museum, Chichester, (center left) Mathew Ward © Dorling Kindersley; **Unit and chapter openers** (background) Reginald Wickham; **Page 1** (top left) David Young-Wolff/PhotoEdit, (right) Bill Aron/PhotoEdit, (bottom left) Shutterstock; **Page 2** Reuters/Corbis; **Page 28** (left) Visions of America, LLC/Alamy, (right) Alon Reininger/Contact Press Images; **Page 58** Hill Street Studios/Jupiterimages; **Page 84** Shutterstock; **Page 96** Moderately Confused copyright Newspaper Enterprise Association Inc.; **Page 112** (left) Ken Chernus/Getty Images, (top right) First Light/age fotostock, (bottom right) Digital Vision Ltd./SuperStock; **Page 142** (top left) Comstock Images/ Jupiterimages, (top middle) Dreamstime.com, (top right) Shutterstock, (bottom left) Shutterstock, (bottom middle) Shutterstock, (bottom right) Blend Images/Jupiterimages.